MW00396908

CREATIVE SOURDOUGH COOKING

ROSE CANTRELL

WEATHERVANE
BOOKS

Copyright © 1977 by Ottenheimer Publishers, Inc.
All rights reserved.
Library of Congress catalog card number: 77-77130
ISBN: 0-517-23128X
Published under arrangement with Ottenheimer Publishers, Inc.
Printed in the United States of America.

contents

introduction

The discovery of sourdough is described both in historical accounts of Columbus' discovery of America and in tales of the Gold Rush era. Writers of American history credit Columbus with the discovery of sourdough. They claim he discovered this "wonder" when his flour supply became saturated with seawater during his voyage to discover the New World.

The story goes that Columbus' men discovered a sour odor coming from the storage room in the hull of the ship. Investigating the problem, the men found that the flour sacks had become soaked with water during the last sea storm. Columbus, knowing that his sailors could not survive if the flour was thrown overboard, ordered his cook to find some way to use the seemingly spoiled flour. Fully expecting to be thrown overboard by the crew, the cook used the "spoiled" flour to bake bread, in an attempt to disguise the taste. To the cook's amazement and delight, the spoiled flour had rising capabilities as well as a delicious taste—thus, the birth of sourdough bread.

However, if you listen to the yarn-spinners reliving the "Old West," they would bet "their bottom dollar" that sourdough starter was created by the miners of the Gold Rush era. These story-tellers lay claim to the strains that are still used in California today.

In their version of the creation of sourdough starter, since the miners did not have access to modern conveniences such as a general store, they would make a batch of biscuits for breakfast and save one biscuit in a sack to give rise to the batch of biscuits at the next meal. This, they say, was the development of sourdough starter.

Today the interest in sourdough cooking is growing in response to the back-to-nature trend that our society is experiencing. We are beginning to feel that perhaps some of our forefathers' innovations need not be improved on too much to make life better for mankind.

sourdough starters

Regardless of who invented the sourdough starter, the original recipes documented in either account give the following recipe for making sourdough starter.

2 cups flour
2 cups water

Combine the flour and water and let the mixture set in a warm place until soured. You will know when it is sour by the bubbling action and the smell. (As the miners would say: "You'll know when she's up.")

When starter is used, save a little to make the next batch. Add flour and water to the saved starter to obtain the original consistency. Keep it in a warm place.

The prairie wife kept her starter hanging behind the old wood stove. She used it every day and did not have to worry about it spoiling.

There is no mysterious secret to the starter process. The warm flour-and-water mixture provides an ideal home for the yeasts in the air to live and multiply. Once the yeast colonies begin to grow, their multiplication is the reason for the starter action and smell.

You may have difficulty today in getting yeast colonies to grow in modern homes, especially those surrounded by asphalt, concrete, and newly turned earth. Yeast colonies are living creatures, and, just like man, they prefer to grow and multiply where they can put down roots. Because of the constant building-and-tearing-down trend in this modern world, yeast colonies are not as plentiful in today's environment as they were in the days of our forefathers. If you happen to live in a 100-year-old farmhouse surrounded by undisturbed vegetation, you will probably have no trouble getting sourdough starter to work by using flour and water. However, if you are like the majority of Americans, who do not live in such stable conditions, you will probably have to use commercial yeast to get your sourdough to work effectively. In addition, when your starter begins to act, it will not rise bread to the desired height most of us are accustomed to in baked bread. Therefore, this book has included a package of commercial yeast in each recipe that uses yeast as the rising agent. You will have to experiment with your starter to determine its rising capabilities. Be brave — *experiment!*

Over the years cooks and homemakers have added their own variations to the original sourdough-starter recipe. The following recipes are the most popular used to create sourdough starter.

sourdough starter I

The original recipe for sourdough starter.

2 cups warm water
2 cups all-purpose white flour

Using a stone jar or crock, combine the water and flour. Place mixture in warm place for 3 to 4 days, until it is bubbly and smells sour; then refrigerate the starter.

sourdough starter II

1 package active dry yeast
2 cups warm water
2 cups all-purpose white flour

Using a stone jar or crock, dissolve the yeast in the warm water. Stir in the flour. Place mixture in warm place for 3 to 4 days or until it is bubbly and smells sour, then refrigerate it.

sourdough starter III

The milk in this starter will add extra nutrients to your baked goods.

2 cups milk
2 cups all-purpose white flour

Pour the milk into a stone jar or crock. Let set at room temperature for 2 days, until really sour. Add the flour. Let mixture set in warm place for 1 to 2 days, until it is bubbly and smells sour. Refrigerate it. (After using starter, remember to replenish the liquid with milk instead of water.)

sourdough starter IV

Some bakers add the sugar to give the yeast cells additional food.

1 package active dry yeast
2 cups warm water
2 cups flour
2 tablespoons granulated sugar

Using a stone jar or crock, dissolve the yeast in the warm water. Add the flour and sugar. Place mixture in warm place for 3 to 4 days or until it is bubbly and smells sour. Refrigerate it.

sourdough starter V

This starter is for true lovers of the strong sour flavor.

1 package active dry yeast
2 cups warm water
2 tablespoons vinegar
2 cups all-purpose white flour

Using a stone jar or crock, dissolve the yeast in the warm water. Add the vinegar. Stir in the flour. Let mixture stand in warm place for 3 to 4 days or until it is bubbly and smells sour. Refrigerate it.

hints for successful sourdough-baking

1) All ingredients must be at least at room temperature to enable the starter to work effectively. Cold ingredients slow down the starter's action.

2) The recipes in this cookbook instruct you to rise the sponge overnight or for 12 hours. The purpose of this time period is to allow the sour flavor and yeast to grow. If you have added commercial yeast and prefer a milder flavor, reduce this time period to 2 hours.

3) When removing starter from your jar for use in a recipe, always add back flour and water to form the original consistency. Let it set at room temperature for 3 to 4 hours or until the mixture bubbles. Refrigerate it.

4) If your starter separates during storage, just stir it and it is ready to use.

5) Starter will keep in the refrigerator for about 6 months. If it is not used by this time, divide the starter and add additional flour and water to form the original consistency.

6) *Always* make starter in a glass or crock jar. *Never make or store starter in a metal container: The starter will react with the metal container.*

yeast breads

french bread

french bread

Yield: 2 loaves

> 1 package active dry yeast
> 1½ cups warm water
> 1 cup sourdough starter
> 1½ cups all-purpose white flour
> 3 tablespoons granulated sugar
> 2 teaspoons salt
> 4½ to 5 cups all-purpose white flour
> ¼ cup yellow cornmeal

Dissolve the yeast in the warm water. Stir in the sourdough starter, blending well. Add the 1½ cups flour. Mix well. Let mixture rise overnight or about 12 hours to develop the sponge.

Stir down the sponge. Add the sugar and salt; mix well. Add 3 to 3½ cups flour to sponge mixture. Work it in. Pour remaining flour onto kneading surface. Pour sponge mixture on top of the flour. Knead until all flour has been worked into the dough. Continue kneading until folds form in dough (about 10 minutes).

Place dough in a greased bowl. Grease the top of the dough. Cover it. Let rise in warm place until doubled in bulk. Punch it down.

Turn the dough onto a lightly floured board. Divide it into 2 equal portions. Roll each portion into a 15 × 10-inch oblong. Beginning at the widest side, roll it up tightly. Pinch the edges together. Taper the ends by gently rolling the dough back and forth. Place the loaves on greased baking sheets sprinkled with cornmeal. Cover; let rise in warm place about 1 hour, or until doubled in bulk.

With a sharp razor make diagonal cuts on top of each loaf. Place loaves in a cold oven in which a pan of boiling water has been placed. Set oven at 450°F and bake loaves about 35 minutes or until a golden crust has formed. Remove them from oven. Cool them on a wire rack.

sourdough white bread

Yield: 1 loaf

1 package active dry yeast
2 cups warm water
½ cup sourdough starter
2 cups all-purpose white flour
2 tablespoons honey
1 teaspoon salt
3 tablespoons margarine,
      melted
4 to 4½ cups all-purpose white
      flour

Dissolve the yeast in the warm water. Add the sourdough starter. Blend thoroughly. Mix in the 2 cups flour. Cover mixture. Set it in warm place for 12 hours or overnight.

Stir the sponge to dissolve the crust that has formed. Add the honey, salt, and margarine to the sponge, mixing well. Add flour until a soft dough has formed.

Pour remaining flour on kneading surface and work it into the dough. Knead for about 10 minutes or until folds form in the dough ball.

Place dough ball in a greased bowl. Grease the top. Cover and let it rise until doubled in bulk. Punch it down. Knead for 2 minutes. Shape it into a loaf and place in a greased pan. Let rise until the top of the loaf rises above the rim of the pan. Place in cold oven. Set oven at 375°F. Bake loaf 60 minutes or until done.

Remove the loaf from the pan. Brush the top with oil. Cool it on a rack. Store loaf in a plastic bag to maintain freshness.

italian herb bread

Yield: 1 9-inch loaf

1 package active dry yeast
2 cups warm water
½ cup sourdough starter
2 cups all-purpose white flour
2 tablespoons granulated sugar
1 teaspoon salt
¼ cup shortening, melted
4 to 4½ cups all-purpose white
    flour
¼ cup margarine, melted
½ package Italian
    salad-dressing mix
1 teaspoon parsley flakes
½ teaspoon oregano
1 egg, beaten
2 tablespoons sesame seeds

Dissolve the yeast in the warm water. Add the sourdough starter. Mix in the 2 cups flour. Cover mixture. Let it set for 12 hours or overnight to develop the sponge.

Stir the sponge to dissolve the crust. Add the sugar, salt, and shortening; mix well. Add flour until a soft dough has formed.

Pour 1 cup flour onto kneading surface. Pour the sponge on top of the flour. Knead it in. Add enough of remaining flour to develop a medium-stiff dough. Knead for 10 minutes or until folds appear in dough.

Place the dough ball in a greased bowl. Grease the top of the ball. Cover it. Let rise until doubled in bulk. Punch it down. Knead for 2 minutes. Roll dough into a 10 × 12-inch rectangle. Spread dough with the melted margarine.

Mix together the Italian dressing mix, parsley flakes, and oregano. Sprinkle mixture over the margarine. Roll up dough as for a jelly roll. Fold in the ends and place dough into a 9-inch greased loaf pan. Cover it. Let rise until the dough crown comes above the pan rim. Brush the crown with beaten egg; sprinkle with sesame seeds. Place in cold oven. Set oven at 375°F. Bake dough approximately 1 hour, or until done. Remove it from pan to cool.

pepperoni loaf

pepperoni loaf

Yield: 1 9-inch loaf

1 package compressed yeast
1 cup warm water
1 cup sourdough starter
3 cups unbleached white flour
2 tablespoons granulated sugar
1 teaspoon salt
¼ teaspoon garlic powder
3 tablespoons oil
8 ounces hard pepperoni,
    chopped fine
3 to 3½ cups unbleached
    white flour
1 egg, beaten

Dissolve the yeast in the warm water. Add the sourdough starter. Blend thoroughly. Mix in 1 cup flour. Cover. Let mixture set overnight or for 12 hours to develop the sponge.

Stir to dissolve the crust. Add the sugar, salt, garlic powder, and oil to the sponge. Stir to blend. Work in 2 more cups flour. Add the pepperoni. Work it into the dough.

Pour 1 cup of remaining flour onto kneading surface. Pour sponge mixture on top of flour. Cover sponge with 1 cup of remaining flour. Work the flour into the dough. Add enough remaining flour to make a medium-stiff dough. Knead for about 10 minutes or until folds form in the dough.

Place the dough into a greased bowl. Grease the top. Cover it. Let rise until doubled in bulk. Punch it down. Knead for 2 minutes. Form it into a loaf.

Place dough in a greased 9-inch loaf pan. Let rise until the crown of the bread rises above the pan. Brush top of loaf with beaten egg. Place in cold oven. Set oven at 375°F. Bake dough 60 minutes or until done. Remove it from the pan to cool.

caraway rye loaf

The dough may be formed into 2 smaller loaves.

Yield: 1 oblong loaf

1 cake compressed yeast
2 cups warm water
½ cup sourdough starter
2 cups all-purpose white flour
¼ cup molasses
1 teaspoon salt
3 tablespoons shortening,
   melted
2 tablespoons caraway seeds
4 to 4½ cups rye flour
¼ cup cornmeal
1 egg, beaten

caraway rye loaf

Dissolve the yeast in the warm water. Add the sourdough starter. Blend thoroughly. Mix in 2 cups white flour. Cover mixture. Set it in warm place for 12 hours or overnight.

Stir mixture to dissolve the crust that has formed on top. Add the molasses, salt, shortening, and caraway seeds. Mix well. Add rye flour until a soft dough has formed. Pour 1 cup rye flour on kneading surface. Pour the dough on top of the flour. Knead flour into the dough. Add enough remaining flour to form a medium-stiff dough. Knead for 10 minutes or until folds form in the dough.

Place dough ball in a greased bowl. Grease the top. Cover it. Let rise until doubled in bulk. Punch the dough down. Knead for 2 minutes. Form dough into an oblong loaf.

Place loaf on greased cookie sheet that has been dusted with ¼ cup of cornmeal. Cover it. Let rise until doubled in bulk.

Place loaf in a 400°F oven for 10 minutes. Remove it from the oven. Brush with beaten egg. Return it to the oven. Bake it an additional 35 to 40 minutes or until done. Cool it on a rack.

whole-wheat molasses bread

Yield: 1 9-inch loaf

1 package active dry yeast
1½ cups warm water
½ cup sourdough starter
4 cups all-purpose white flour
½ cup milk

2 tablespoons molasses
2 tablespoons oil
1 teaspoon salt
2 cups whole-wheat flour

Dissolve the yeast in the warm water. Stir in the sourdough starter. Add 2 cups all-purpose white flour. Let mixture set for 12 hours or overnight to develop the sponge.

Stir down the sponge. Add the milk, molasses, oil, and salt; mix well. Add the remaining 2 cups flour; stir until moistened.

Spread 1 cup whole-wheat flour on kneading surface. Pour sponge mixture on top of the flour. Knead in the flour. Add enough remaining flour to develop a medium-stiff dough. Knead dough for 10 minutes or until elastic.

Place the dough in a greased bowl. Grease the top. Cover and let it rise until doubled in bulk.

Punch down the dough. Knead for 2 minutes. Shape it into a loaf and place into greased 9-inch loaf pan. Let rise until doubled in bulk.

Place the loaf in a cold oven. Set oven at 375°F. Bake loaf 1 hour or until done.

coffee-can cheese bread

Yield: 1 loaf

½ cup milk
¼ cup margarine
1 box hot-roll mix
½ cup sourdough starter

1 egg, beaten
1 cup cheddar cheese, grated
¼ cup margarine, melted

Heat the milk and margarine to lukewarm. Dissolve the yeast from the hot-roll mix in the warm liquid. Stir in the sourdough starter and egg. Add flour mixture from hot-roll mix. Blend well. Cover. Let rise until doubled in bulk.

Punch down the dough. Knead in the cheddar cheese.

Grease a 2-pound coffee can. Form dough into a ball. Place in coffee can; flatten dough slightly. Cover. Let rise until doubled in bulk.

Preheat oven to 375°F. Bake loaf 30 to 40 minutes, until deep golden brown and the can sounds hollow when lightly tapped. Brush top with melted margarine. Remove loaf from can to cool.

banana wheat bread

This bread makes a delicious breakfast toast.

Yield: 1 loaf

1 package active dry yeast
¼ cup warm water
1 cup sourdough starter
1 teaspoon salt
¼ cup wheat germ
2 tablespoons honey
3 tablespoons oil
1 cup very ripe bananas,
mashed
2 cups all-purpose white flour
2½ to 3 cups whole-wheat
flour
2 tablespoons melted butter

Dissolve the yeast in the warm water. Add the starter to the yeast mixture.

Combine the salt, wheat germ, honey, oil, and bananas with a wooden spoon. Mix together on low speed in electric mixer until well-blended. Add the all-purpose white flour to banana mixture and continue to beat on low speed until blended. Beat in the yeast mixture. Add the whole-wheat flour gradually. Mix it in thoroughly.

Turn the dough onto floured board. Knead for 10 minutes.

Place the dough in an oiled bowl. Oil the top of the dough. Cover it with a damp towel. Set it in warm place and let rise until doubled in bulk.

Punch down the dough. Turn it onto a floured board and knead for 2 minutes. Shape dough into 1 loaf. Place in an oiled bread pan. Let rise until doubled in bulk.

Bake at 350°F for 50 minutes or until done. Brush baked loaf with melted butter.

biblical bread

Yield: 2 8-inch-round loaves

½ cup lukewarm milk
½ cup lukewarm water
1 package active dry yeast
1¾ teaspoons salt

1 cup sourdough starter
2 cups barley flour
2¼ cups all-purpose white
flour

Combine the milk and water. Add the yeast and salt. Stir until dissolved. Mix in the sourdough starter. Add the barley flour. Mix well. Cover mixture. Let rise until doubled in bulk.

Punch down the dough. Add the white flour. Mix until smooth. Let rise for 30 minutes.

Punch down the dough. Knead it until smooth. Divide it into 2 parts. Shape it into 2 8-inch-round loaves. Place loaves on greased baking sheets. Let rise until doubled in bulk. Prick tops with a fork.

Bake loaves in preheated 400°F oven 15 to 20 minutes or until done. Let them cool.

honey whole-wheat bread

Yield: 1 9-inch loaf

1 package active dry yeast
2 cups warm water
½ cup sourdough starter
4 cups unbleached white flour
¼ cup honey

2 tablespoons margarine,
melted
1 teaspoon salt
2 to 2½ cups whole-wheat
flour

Dissolve the yeast in the warm water. Stir in the sourdough starter and 2 cups unbleached white flour. Let mixture set for 12 hours or overnight to develop the sponge.

Stir down the sponge to dissolve the crust. Add the honey, margarine, and salt. Mix well. Add remaining 2 cups white flour. Stir until flour is moistened.

Spread 1 cup whole-wheat flour on kneading surface. Pour sponge mixture on top of the flour. Knead in the flour. Add enough remaining flour to develop a medium-stiff dough. Knead dough for 10 minutes or until elastic.

Place the dough in a greased bowl. Grease the top. Cover it. Let rise until doubled in bulk.

Punch down the dough. Knead for 2 minutes. Shape it into a loaf and place into greased 9-inch loaf pan. Let rise until doubled in bulk.

Place loaf in cold oven. Set oven at 375°F. Bake loaf 1 hour or until done. Remove it from pan to cool.

raisin whole-wheat bread

Yield: 1 9-inch loaf

> **1 package active dry yeast**
> **1 cup warm water**
> **1 cup sourdough starter**
> **3 cups all-purpose white flour**
> **½ cup water**
> **2 tablespoons molasses**
> **2 tablespoons shortening,**
> **melted**
> **1 teaspoon salt**
> **1 cup raisins**
> **3 to 3½ cups whole-wheat**
> **flour**

Soften the yeast in the warm water. Add the sourdough starter. Stir in 1 cup white flour. Cover it. Let rise in warm place for 12 hours or overnight to develop the sponge.

Stir the sponge to dissolve the crust. Add ½ cup water, the molasses, shortening, and salt. Stir them in. Work in remaining 2 cups white flour. Add the raisins. Work them in.

Pour 1 cup whole-wheat flour on top of kneading surface. Pour sponge mixture on top of the flour. Cover with 1 cup whole-wheat flour. Knead until flour is worked into the dough. Continue adding flour until a stiff dough has formed. Knead dough 10 minutes or until folds form in it.

Place the dough in a greased bowl. Grease the top of dough ball. Cover it. Let rise until doubled in bulk.

Punch down the dough ball. Knead for 2 minutes. Form dough into a loaf. Place loaf in greased 9-inch loaf pan. Cover it. Let rise until the bread crown rises above the pan rim.

Place loaf in a cool oven. Set oven at 375°F and bake bread 1 hour or until done. Remove it from oven and place on a rack to cool.

yeast-rising cornbread

Yield: 6 servings

1 cup milk
1 package active dry yeast
½ cup sourdough starter
2 eggs, beaten
3 tablespoons granulated sugar

3 tablespoons shortening,
    melted
1 cup cornmeal
¾ cup all-purpose white flour
1 teaspoon salt

Scald the milk. Cook it until lukewarm.

Soften the yeast in the milk. Add the sourdough starter. Let mixture stand for 10 minutes.

Add remaining ingredients. Pour mixture into a greased 8-inch-diameter cast-iron skillet. Set it in warm place. Let it rise for 30 minutes.

Bake the cornbread at 350°F for 30 minutes. Serve it warm.

syrian bread

Yield: 2-dozen rolls

1 package active dry yeast
2 cups warm water
½ cup sourdough starter
2 cups unbleached white flour
¼ cup honey

2 tablespoons margarine,
    melted
2 teaspoons salt
3½ to 4 cups unbleached
    white flour

Dissolve the yeast in the warm water. Stir in the sourdough starter, blending well. Add the 2 cups flour. Mix well. Let mixture rise overnight or about 12 hours to develop the sponge.

Stir down the sponge. Add the honey, margarine, and salt; blend them in. Add approximately 3 cups flour — enough to form a stiff dough.

Pour remaining flour onto kneading surface. Pour the bread sponge on top of the flour. Knead until all flour has been worked into the dough. Continue kneading until dough is smooth and elastic. Place in greased bowl, remembering to grease the top. Cover it. Let rise until doubled in bulk.

Punch down the dough. Cover it with the bowl and let rest for 10 minutes. Form dough into balls about 2 inches in diameter. Place balls on ungreased cookie sheet. Pat them to a flat circle 4 inches in diameter.

Place the dough balls in a preheated 400°F oven and bake them 8 minutes or until puffed. Cool them wrapped in a cloth to retain softness.

cuban rounds

Yield: 2 round loaves

1 package active dry yeast
2 cups warm water
½ cup sourdough starter
2 cups all-purpose white flour
2½ tablespoons honey
2 teaspoons salt
3½ to 4 cups all-purpose flour
Ice water

Dissolve the yeast in the warm water. Stir in the sourdough starter. Blend well. Add 2 cups flour. Mix well. Let dough rise overnight or 12 hours to develop the sponge.

Stir down the sponge. Add the honey and salt to the sponge; mix well. Stir 2 to 3 cups flour into sponge mixture.

Pour remaining flour onto kneading surface. Pour sponge mixture on top of the flour. Knead until all flour has been worked into sponge mixture. Continue kneading until dough is smooth and elastic (about 10 minutes).

Place the dough in a greased bowl. Grease the top. Cover dough. Let rise until doubled in bulk.

Punch down the dough. Turn it out onto kneading surface; invert the bowl over the dough; let rest for 10 minutes.

Divide the dough in half and knead each piece for 2 minutes. Form each dough ball into an 8-inch circle by patting the dough in a circular motion. Place the circles on greased cookie sheets and let rise in warm place free from draft until doubled in bulk.

Slit tops of each loaf in a tic-tac-toe design with a sharp razor blade, making the slits approximately 2 inches apart. Brush loaves with ice water.

Place the loaves in a cold oven. Set oven at 400°F and bake the rounds approximately 40 minutes, brushing each loaf with ice water several times during baking period. Remove them from oven and cool them on wire rack. If not used within 2 days, freeze rounds to retain freshness.

turkish
turban

Yield: 1 loaf

> 1 package active dry yeast
> 2 cups warm water
> ½ cup sourdough starter
> 2 cups all-purpose white flour
> 2 tablespoons honey
> 1 teaspoon salt
> 3 tablespoons shortening,
>   melted
> 4½ to 5 cups all-purpose white
>   flour
> 1 cup raisins
> 1 egg, beaten

turkish turban

Dissolve the yeast in the warm water. Add the sourdough starter. Blend thoroughly. Mix in 2 cups flour. Cover mixture. Set it in a warm place for 12 hours or overnight.

Stir the sponge to dissolve the crust that has formed. Add the honey, salt, and shortening to the sponge. Mix well. Add flour until a soft dough has formed.

Pour remaining flour on kneading surface. Work flour into dough. Knead about 10 minutes or until folds form in dough. Place dough ball in greased bowl. Grease the top. Cover it. Let rise until doubled in bulk.

Punch down the dough. Knead the raisins into the dough. Divide dough into 2 equal parts. Form 1 part into a ball. Place on a greased cookie sheet. Flatten top slightly. Form remaining dough into a cylinder long enough to wrap around first dough ball. Pinch edges together so that cylinder fits tightly around dough ball. Cover it. Let rise until doubled in bulk. Brush loaf with beaten egg. Place in cold oven. Set oven at 375°F. Bake loaf 60 minutes or until done. Cool it on a rack.

egg braid

Yield: 2 braids

1 package active dry yeast
1 cup warm water
1 cup sourdough starter
1 cup all-purpose white flour
⅓ cup granulated sugar
2 eggs, beaten
½ cup butter, melted
1 teaspoon salt
4 to 4½ cups all-purpose white
     flour
2 eggs, beaten

Dissolve the yeast in the warm water. Add the sourdough starter. Mix in 1 cup flour. Let mixture set for 12 hours or overnight to develop the sponge.

Stir the sponge to dissolve the crust. Add the sugar, 2 beaten eggs, butter, and salt. Mix well. Add 2½ cups flour to the sponge. Mix well.

Pour 1 cup flour on kneading surface. Pour sponge mixture on top of the flour. Cover with 1 cup flour. Knead until the flour is worked into dough. Continue adding flour until a stiff dough has formed. Knead dough for 10 minutes or until folds form in it. Place in greased bowl. Grease the top. Cover it. Let rise until doubled in bulk.

Punch down the dough. Knead for 2 more minutes. Divide dough into 2 equal balls. Divide 1 dough ball again into 8 equal parts. Roll the 8 parts until approximately 12 inches long. Place these 8 strips side-by-side and braid them by folding 1 strip over the other in numerical order. Tuck in the edges. Prepare the second dough ball in the same manner. Place braids on greased cookie sheets. Cover them. Let rise until doubled in bulk.

Brush braids with 2 beaten eggs. Bake them in preheated 350°F oven for 30 minutes or until golden brown. Remove them from oven and brush them with oil. Cool them on a rack.

Picture on opposite page: egg braid

dinner rolls

pan rolls

Yield: 15 rolls

½ cup milk
¼ cup margarine
1 box hot-roll mix
½ cup sourdough starter
1 egg, beaten
¼ cup margarine, melted

pan rolls

Heat the milk and ¼ cup margarine to lukewarm. Dissolve the yeast from hot-roll mix in the warm liquid. Stir in the sourdough starter and egg. Add flour mixture from hot-roll mix. Blend well. Cover mixture. Let rise until doubled in bulk.

Punch down the dough. Knead it on floured surface until no longer sticky.

Grease a 13 × 9-inch pan. Divide dough into 15 equal pieces and shape the pieces into balls. Place in a pan and cover it. Let rise again until double in size.

Bake the balls in a preheated 375°F oven for 18 to 25 minutes or until golden brown. Brush the warm rolls with melted margarine.

quick sourdough dinner rolls

Yield: 1 dozen

1 box hot-roll mix
1 cup warm water
1 egg, beaten

1 package sour-cream mix
(1.25 ounces)
¼ cup margarine, melted

Dissolve the yeast from the roll mix in the warm water. Add beaten egg. Blend well.

Combine sour-cream-sauce mix with flour from hot-roll mix. Add to yeast mixture; blend well. Cover mixture and let rise in warm place until doubled in bulk.

Punch down the dough. Knead it on floured surface until it is not sticky. Shape it into 16 equal pieces.

Grease a 13 × 9-inch pan. Shape dough pieces into balls. Place in a pan, and cover. Let rise until doubled in bulk.

Bake the balls in a preheated 375°F oven for 20 minutes or until done. Brush the warm rolls with melted margarine.

no-knead dinner rolls

Yield: 1½ dozen

3 cups unbleached white flour
1 package active dry yeast
¾ cup milk
½ cup margarine
¼ cup granulated sugar
1 teaspoon salt
1 cup sourdough starter
1 egg, beaten
¼ cup margarine, melted

In a large mixing bowl combine 2 cups of flour and the yeast. Mix until well-blended.

Scald the milk. Pour it over the margarine, sugar, and salt. Stir until margarine melts and sugar and salt are dissolved. Cool mixture to lukewarm.

Add the milk mixture and the sourdough starter to the flour-and-yeast mixture. Add the egg. Beat on low speed of electric mixer for 1 minute. Proceed to high speed and beat 3 minutes. Add remaining 1 cup flour. Set mixer on medium speed. Beat 3 minutes more or until batter is smooth. (The batter will stick to the beaters at this point.) Cover mixing bowl and put it in warm place until batter is doubled in bulk.

Stir down the batter. Beat it thoroughly by hand. Drop batter by heaping tablespoons into greased muffin tins. Let rise until doubled in bulk.

Place the rolls in a cold oven. Set oven at 400°F and bake rolls 20 minutes or until done. Remove them from muffin tins immediately. Grease the tops with melted margarine.

easy whole-wheat dinner rolls

Yield: 18 rolls

    1½ cups all-purpose white
        flour
    ½ cup whole-wheat flour
    1 package active dry yeast
    ¼ cup dry milk powder
    ¾ cup warm water
    ½ cup shortening, melted
    ¼ cup molasses
    1 teaspoon salt
    1 cup sourdough starter
    1 egg, beaten
    ¾ to 1 cup whole-wheat flour

In a large mixing bowl combine the white flour, ½ cup whole-wheat flour, the yeast, and the dry milk powder. Mix well. Add the warm water, melted shortening, molasses, salt, sourdough starter, and egg to flour mixture. Beat on low speed of electric mixer for 1 minute. Proceed to high speed and beat for 3 minutes. Add remaining flour. Set mixer on medium speed. Beat for 3 minutes more or until batter is smooth. The batter will stick to beaters at this point. If it does not, add more whole-wheat flour until dough does stick to beaters. Cover mixing bowl and put it in warm place until batter has doubled in bulk.

Stir down the batter. Beat it thoroughly by hand. Drop batter by heaping tablespoons into greased muffin tins. Let rise in warm place until doubled in bulk.

Place the muffin tins in a cold oven. Set oven at 400°F and bake rolls 20 to 25 minutes or until done. Remove them from pans immediately. Brush the tops with water.

rye rolls

Yield: 2 dozen

1 package active dry yeast
2 cups warm water (105 to
  115°F)
½ cup Sourdough Starter II
2 cups all-purpose white flour
2 tablespoons molasses
1 teaspoon salt
3 tablespoons margarine,
  melted
4 to 4½ cups light rye flour
½ cup margarine, melted

Dissolve the yeast in the warm water. Add the sourdough starter. Blend thoroughly. Mix in the white flour. Cover mixture. Set it in warm place for 12 hours or overnight. (A crust will cover the starter.)

Stir the sponge to dissolve the crust. Add the molasses, salt, and the 3 tablespoons melted margarine to the sponge. Mix well. Add rye flour until a soft dough has formed (about 3½ to 4 cups). Pour remaining flour onto kneading surface. Work it into the dough. Knead about 10 minutes or until folds form in dough ball. Place dough ball in greased bowl. Grease the top. Cover bowl. Let dough rise until doubled in bulk.

Punch down the dough. Knead for another 2 minutes. Take a piece of dough (about ¼ cup) from kneaded ball and shape it into an oblong roll. Continue this process until 2-dozen rolls are formed. Place rolls on greased cookie sheet. Put in warm place and let double in bulk.

Place the rolls in a cold oven. Turn oven on, setting it at 375°F. Bake rolls 20 minutes or until done. Remove them from pan. Brush the tops with ½ cup melted margarine.

brioches

Yield: 2 dozen

1 package active dry yeast
1 cup warm water
1 cup sourdough starter
1 cup all-purpose white flour
½ cup sugar
1 cup butter, melted

1 teaspoon salt
5 eggs, beaten
5 to 5½ cups all-purpose white
  flour
1 egg, beaten
1 tablespoon water

Dissolve the yeast in the warm water. Add the sourdough starter. Blend thoroughly. Mix in 1 cup flour. Cover mixture. Let stand overnight.

Stir the sponge to dissolve the crust. Add the sugar, butter, salt, and 5 eggs; mix well. Add enough remaining flour to make a soft dough. Turn it out onto floured pastry cloth and knead until dough is smooth. Place it in greased bowl, cover, and let rise until doubled in bulk.

Punch down the dough and divide it into 24 equal parts. Cut a small piece of dough from each of the 24 pieces. Shape the large pieces of dough into round balls and place in greased brioche pans or greased muffin tins. Make an indentation in the center of each large ball. Form the small pieces of dough into balls, and place them in the indentations in the large balls. Cover balls. Let rise until doubled in bulk.

Mix the egg and water. Brush brioches with mixture.

Bake brioches in preheated 375°F oven 15 minutes or until golden brown. Cool them on racks.

brioches

29

hard rolls

Yield: 3-dozen rolls

1 package active dry yeast
1½ cups warm water
1 cup sourdough starter
1½ cups all-purpose white
    flour
3 tablespoons granulated sugar
2 teaspoons salt
4½ to 5 cups all-purpose white
    flour
½ cup yellow cornmeal

Dissolve the yeast in the warm water. Stir in the sourdough starter, blending well. Add 1½ cups flour; mix well. Let mixture rise overnight or about 12 hours to develop the sourdough sponge.

Stir down the sponge. Add the sugar and salt to the sponge; mix well. Add 3½ cups flour to sponge mixture.

Pour remaining flour onto kneading surface. Pour sponge mixture on top of the flour. Knead until all flour has been worked into sponge mixture. Continue kneading until folds form in dough (about 10 minutes). Place dough in greased bowl. Grease the top. Cover bowl. Let dough rise until doubled in bulk.

Punch down the dough. Turn it onto lightly floured board; divide it into 3-dozen balls. With floured hands roll each ball until it is 4 inches long. Between your hands roll the ends to taper them.

Sprinkle greased cookie sheets with cornmeal. Place rolls on top of cornmeal. Cover them. Let rise until doubled in bulk.

With a sharp razor make diagonal cuts on top of each roll. Put rolls in cold oven in which a pan of boiling water has been placed. Set oven at 450°F and bake rolls 15 minutes or until golden crusts have formed.

crescent rolls

Yield: 27 rolls

1 cake compressed yeast
1 cup warm water
½ cup sourdough starter
⅓ cup nonfat dry milk
1 cup all-purpose white flour
½ cup shortening, melted
½ cup granulated sugar
2 eggs, beaten
1 teaspoon salt
3½ to 4½ cups all-purpose
    white flour
½ cup margarine, melted

crescent rolls

Dissolve the yeast in the warm water. Add the sourdough starter; mix well. Add the nonfat dry milk and 1 cup flour. Cover mixture. Let stand overnight to develop the sponge.

Stir down the sponge to dissolve the crust. Add the shortening, sugar, eggs, and salt; mix well. Add enough remaining flour to make a soft dough.

Turn out the dough onto a floured surface and knead until dough is smooth. Place it in greased bowl, cover, and let rise until doubled in bulk.

Punch down the dough and divide it into thirds. On floured surface roll each third to a 9-inch circle. Brush the circles with melted margarine. Cut each circle into 9 equal wedges. Roll each wedge, starting with the wide end. Place on greased cookie sheet. Put the ends of the wedges on the bottom to prevent rolls from unrolling. Curve ends of rolls to form crescent shapes. Cover them. Let rise until doubled in bulk.

Bake in preheated 400°F oven 10 to 12 minutes or until rolls are golden brown.

whole-wheat parkerhouse rolls

Yield: 2½ dozen

1 package active dry yeast
2 cups warm water
½ cup sourdough starter
2 cups all-purpose white flour
¼ cup granulated sugar
2 tablespoons shortening,
    melted
1 teaspoon salt
2 cups unbleached white flour
2 to 2½ cups whole-wheat
    flour
½ cup butter, melted

Dissolve the yeast in the warm water. Stir in the sourdough starter. Add 2 cups all-purpose white flour. Let mixture set overnight to develop the sponge.

Stir down the sponge to dissolve the crust. Add the sugar, shortening, and salt; mix well. Add the 2 cups of unbleached white flour. Stir until it is moistened.

Spread 1 cup of the whole-wheat flour on kneading surface. Pour sponge mixture on top of the flour. Knead in the flour. Add enough remaining flour to develop a medium-stiff dough. Knead for 10 minutes or until dough is elastic. Place in greased bowl. Grease the top. Cover dough. Let rise until doubled in bulk.

Punch down the dough. Knead for 2 minutes. Roll dough ¼ inch thick on lightly floured board. Cut it in rounds with a 2½-inch floured biscuit- or cookie-cutter. Brush with melted butter. With the back of a table knife make a crease in each round just off center. Fold the larger side of each round over the other side, overlapping slightly. Seal the end edges. Brush with melted butter. Place rolls about 1 inch apart on greased baking sheet. Cover them. Let rise until doubled in bulk.

Bake at 400°F for 12 to 15 minutes or until golden brown. They are best when served warm.

corn four-leaf clovers

Yield: 2½-dozen rolls

1 package active dry yeast
1 cup warm milk
½ cup sourdough starter
1 cup all-purpose white flour
½ cup shortening, melted
1 teaspoon salt
¼ cup honey
2 eggs, beaten
1 cup cornmeal
2½ to 3 cups all-purpose white
    flour

Dissolve the yeast in the warm milk. Stir in the sourdough starter. Add 1 cup flour; mix well. Let mixture rise overnight or about 12 hours to develop the sponge.

Stir down the sponge. Add the shortening, salt, honey, and eggs; mix well. Stir in the cornmeal. Add enough remaining flour to develop a soft dough.

Turn dough onto floured surface and knead for 10 minutes or until folds form in dough. Place dough in greased bowl. Grease the top. Cover bowl. Let dough rise until doubled in bulk.

Punch down the dough. Knead it 2 minutes. Form it into 2-inch balls. Place in greased muffin tins. With scissors slash the surface of each ball one direction and then across again in the opposite direction to form an "X." Cover balls. Let rise in warm place until doubled in bulk.

Bake rolls in 425°F oven 12 to 15 minutes. Remove them from pans to cool.

cloverleaf rolls

Yield: 24 rolls

1 package active dry yeast
2 cups warm water
½ cup sourdough starter
2 cups unbleached white flour
2 tablespoons granulated sugar
1 teaspoon salt
3 tablespoons shortening,
    melted
4 to 4½ cups unbleached
    white flour
¼ cup margarine, melted

Dissolve the yeast in the warm water. Add the sourdough starter. Blend thoroughly. Mix in 2 cups flour. Cover mixture. Set it in warm place for 12 hours or overnight.

Stir the sponge to dissolve the crust that has formed on top of the starter. Add the sugar, salt, and melted shortening to the sponge; mix well. Add flour until a soft dough has formed (about 3½ to 4 cups).

Pour remaining flour on kneading surface. Work it into the dough. Knead for 10 minutes or until folds form in dough ball. Place dough ball in greased bowl. Grease the top of dough ball. Cover it and let rise until doubled in bulk.

Punch down the dough ball. Knead another 2 minutes.

Generously grease 2 12-cup muffin tins. Pinch off small pieces of dough and shape them into small balls, rolling them between your palms until they are about ½ inch in diameter. Arrange 3 balls closely together in each muffin cup. Cover the tins with a cloth and let dough rise in warm place about 25 minutes or until each roll reaches the top of the pan.

Brush roll tops with melted butter. Bake them 10 to 15 minutes in a 425°F oven. Remove rolls from muffin tins. Serve them warm.

butterhorns

Yield: 27 rolls

   1 package active dry yeast
   ¾ cup warm milk
   ½ cup sourdough starter
   1 cup all-purpose white flour
   ½ cup butter, melted
   ½ cup honey
   2 eggs, beaten
   1 teaspoon salt
   3½ to 4 cups all-purpose white
      flour
   ½ cup butter, melted

Dissolve the yeast in the warm milk. Add the sourdough starter. Blend thoroughly. Mix in 1 cup flour. Cover mixture. Let stand overnight to develop the sponge.

Stir down the sponge to dissolve the crust. Add the butter, honey, eggs, and salt; mix well. Add enough remaining flour to make a soft dough.

Turn out dough onto floured surface and knead until dough is smooth. Place in greased bowl. Cover bowl. Let dough rise until doubled in bulk.

Punch down the dough and divide it into thirds. On floured surface roll each third to a 9-inch circle. Brush the circles with melted butter. Cut each circle into 9 equal wedges. Roll each wedge, starting with the wide end. Place them on greased cookie sheet. Put the ends of the wedges on the bottom to prevent the rolls from unrolling. Cover them. Let rolls double in bulk.

Bake rolls at 325°F for 20 to 25 minutes or until golden brown.

whole-wheat fan-tans

Yield: 3 dozen

1 package active dry yeast
¾ cup warm water
½ cup sourdough starter
3 cups all-purpose white flour
¼ cup shortening, melted
½ cup molasses
2 eggs, beaten
1 teaspoon salt
2 cups whole-wheat flour
½ cup butter, melted

Dissolve the yeast in the warm water. Add the sourdough starter. Blend thoroughly. Mix in 1 cup flour. Cover mixture. Let stand overnight to develop the sponge.

Stir down the sponge to dissolve the crust. Add the shortening, molasses, eggs, and salt; mix well. Add the whole-wheat flour. Add enough remaining white flour to form a medium-soft dough.

Turn out dough onto floured surface and knead 10 minutes or until folds form in dough. Place in greased bowl. Grease the top. Cover dough. Let rise until doubled in bulk.

Punch down the dough. Knead for 2 minutes. Roll dough into a ⅛-inch-thick oblong. Brush it with melted butter. Cut it into 1½-inch-wide strips. Stack 6 strips; cut the stacks into 1½-inch pieces. Place them cut-side-down in greased muffin-pan cups. Cover them. Let rise until doubled in bulk.

Bake fan-tans in preheated 400°F oven 15 to 20 minutes or until browned.

hamburger buns

hamburger buns

Yield: 12 large buns

1 package active dry yeast	**2 teaspoons salt**
2 cups warm water	**¼ cup oil**
½ cup sourdough starter	**2 eggs, beaten**
6 cups all-purpose white flour	**1 cup unprocessed wheat bran**
2 tablespoons honey	**¼ cup margarine, melted**
⅔ cup nonfat dry milk	

Dissolve the yeast in the warm water. Add the sourdough starter. Mix in 2 cups of flour. Let mixture stand 12 hours or overnight to develop the starter.

Stir to dissolve the crust. Add the honey, milk, salt, oil, and eggs to the sponge; mix well. Stir in the bran. Add 2 cups flour to the sponge; work it in.

Pour 1 cup flour on kneading surface. Pour the sponge on top of the flour. Dust the top of dough with flour. Work the flour into the dough. Add remaining flour until a soft dough has formed. Knead for 10 minutes. Place dough ball into a greased bowl. Grease the top of dough ball. Cover the dough. Let rise until doubled in bulk.

Punch down the dough. Knead for 2 minutes. Shape dough into 12 round balls. Place on a greased cookie sheet. Flatten balls slightly. Brush them with melted margarine; cover them. Refrigerate them 2 hours.

Uncover dough balls. Let stand at room temperature 10 minutes.

Bake buns in preheated 400°F oven 20 to 25 minutes or until golden brown. Slice buns before serving them.

zelniky

A cabbage-roll recipe brought to Kansas in 1878 from Czechoslovakia.

Yield: 3 dozen

**1 package active dry yeast
2 cups warm water
½ cup sourdough starter
2 cups unbleached white flour
2 tablespoons granulated sugar
3 teaspoons salt
3 tablespoons margarine,
    melted
4 to 4½ cups unbleached
    white flour
4 pounds cabbage, shredded
    fine
3 tablespoons margarine
1 tablespoon sugar
¼ teaspoon black pepper
½ cup margarine, melted**

Dissolve the yeast in the warm water. Add the sourdough starter. Blend thoroughly. Mix in 2 cups flour. Cover mixture. Set it in warm place for 12 hours or overnight.

Stir the sponge to dissolve the crust that has formed on top of the starter. Add 2 tablespoons sugar, 1 teaspoon salt, and 1 tablespoon melted margarine. Mix well. Add flour until a soft dough has formed.

Pour remaining flour on kneading surface. Work it into the dough. Knead for 10 minutes or until folds form in dough ball. Place dough ball into greased bowl. Grease the top of dough ball. Cover and let it rise until doubled in bulk.

While the bread is rising, wash, remove the core, and shred the cabbage. Add the remaining 2 tablespoons salt, the pepper, and 1 tablespoon sugar; mix well. Squeeze out surplus water from cabbage.

Place ½ cup margarine in deep cookie pan, add the cabbage, and mix well. Spread out the cabbage thinly, place in a moderate oven, and bake cabbage until soft and golden brown, stirring often.

Punch down the dough. Knead for an additional 2 minutes. Pinch off a piece of dough about the size of a Ping-Pong ball. Flatten the ball with your hands to form a 3- to 4-inch circle. Fill the circle with cabbage. Bring the edges together and pinch the seams. Place pinched-side-down on lightly oiled cookie sheet. Do this with rest of dough, making 36 rolls. Let rise for 15 minutes.

Bake rolls at 375°F for 30 minutes or until browned. Grease the tops with melted butter.

sweet dough

strawberry braid

A delicious holiday bread for those who do not care for candied fruit.

Yield: 1 braid

> 1 cake compressed yeast
> ¾ cup warm water
> ½ cup sourdough starter
> 1 cup all-purpose white flour
> ¼ cup sugar
> ¼ cup shortening, melted
> 1 teaspoon salt
> 1 egg, beaten
> 3 to 4 cups all-purpose white
>   flour
> ½ cup strawberry preserves

Dissolve yeast in warm water. Add sourdough starter. Stir in 1 cup flour. Let mixture stand 12 hours or overnight to develop sponge.

Stir to dissolve crust. Add sugar, shortening, salt, and egg; mix. Add 1 cup flour to sponge; mix well. Pour 1 cup flour on top of kneading surface. Pour sponge mixture on top of flour. Cover sponge with ½ cup flour. Knead until flour is worked into dough. Continue adding flour until a soft dough is formed. Knead dough for 10 minutes or until folds form in it. Place in greased bowl. Grease top. Cover dough. Let rise until doubled in bulk.

Punch down dough. Let rest 10 minutes.

Divide dough into 3 pieces. Roll each into a 5 × 15-inch rectangle. Spread ¼ cup strawberry preserves down middle of each rectangle. Roll as for jelly roll; seal firmly. Lay each roll 1 inch apart on greased cookie sheet. Braid by starting in center and working toward each end. Let rise until almost doubled.

Bake braid in 375°F oven 30 minutes. Decorate with Cream Glaze (see Index) if desired.

date braid

Yield: 2 braids

**1 cup dates, pitted and
chopped
¼ cup brown sugar
⅔ cup water
½ cup pecans, chopped
1 tablespoon lemon juice
1 package active dry yeast
1 cup warm milk
½ cup sourdough starter
1 cup all-purpose white flour
1½ teaspoons salt
¼ cup shortening, melted
½ cup granulated sugar
2 eggs, beaten
4 cups all-purpose white flour
1 egg yolk
2 tablespoons milk
2 tablespoons butter
2 tablespoons granulated sugar
⅓ cup all-purpose white flour
½ teaspoon cinnamon**

Combine dates, brown sugar, water, nuts, and lemon juice in saucepan. Bring to a boil over medium heat, stirring constantly, and continue boiling until mixture is thick enough to spread. Cool it.

Dissolve yeast in warm milk. Stir in sourdough starter. Work in 1 cup flour. Cover mixture. Let stand overnight to develop starter.

Stir down sponge. Add salt, shortening, ½ cup sugar, and 2 beaten eggs; mix well. Work in enough remaining flour to make a stiff dough. Knead for 10 minutes or until folds form in dough. Place in greased bowl. Grease top. Cover dough. Let rise until doubled in bulk.

Punch down dough. Knead for 2 minutes. Divide dough in half. Roll out each half into an oblong about 16 × 8 inches. Spread half the date filling down center third of each oblong. Cut 15 slits in the dough along each side of the filling, making strips about 1 inch wide. Fold strips at an angle across filling, alternating from side to side. Place on greased baking sheet. Cover them. Let rise until doubled in bulk.

Brush cakes with mixture of 1 egg yolk and 2 tablespoons milk.

Combine butter, 2 tablespoons sugar, ⅓ cup flour, and the cinnamon. Sprinkle this on top of braids. Bake them in preheated 350°F oven 35 minutes or until golden brown.

lemon–nut round

Yield: 1 loaf

1 package active dry yeast
1 cup warm water
1 cup sourdough starter
1 cup all-purpose white flour
1½ cups granulated sugar
2 eggs, beaten
1½ cups butter, melted
1 teaspoon salt

2 teaspoons lemon peel
4 to 4½ cups all-purpose white
  flour
2 teaspoons cinnamon
¾ cup raisins
1 cup English walnuts,
  chopped

Dissolve yeast in warm water. Add sourdough starter. Mix in 1 cup flour. Let mixture set 12 hours or overnight to develop sponge.

Stir to dissolve crust. Add ½ cup sugar, the eggs, ½ cup butter, the salt, and the lemon peel; mix well. Add 2½ cups flour to sponge; mix well.

Pour 1 cup flour on top of kneading surface. Pour sponge mixture on top of flour. Cover sponge with 1 cup flour. Knead until flour is worked into dough. Continue adding flour until a stiff dough has formed. Knead dough 10 more minutes. Place dough in greased bowl. Grease top of dough. Cover it. Let rise until doubled in bulk.

Punch down dough. Knead for 2 minutes. Roll dough into a 16 × 12-inch rectangle. Spread ½ cup butter on top of ¾ of dough. (Leave a 16 × 3-inch piece of dough plain.)

Combine 1 cup granulated sugar, the cinnamon, raisins, and English walnuts. Spread this evenly over buttered dough. Roll dough as for a jelly roll up to the ¼ plain piece of dough. At this point fold the plain dough under the roll. Place the roll in greased tube pan. Seal edge with a knife. Slit top of roll completely around the circle. Pour ½ cup butter over roll. Cover roll and let rise until doubled in bulk.

Bake roll at 350°F for 45 minutes or until golden brown. Remove it from pan and pour glaze over top. Serve it warm.

glaze

2 cups powdered sugar
1 tablespoon cornstarch
3 tablespoons milk

2 tablespoons warm water
1 teaspoon vanilla

Combine all ingredients; beat well. Pour glaze over Lemon-Nut Round.

Picture on next pages: lemon–nut round

almond stollen

almond stollen

Yield: 3 stollens

1 package active dry yeast
1 cup warm water
1 cup sourdough starter
1 cup unbleached white flour
½ cup honey
2 eggs, beaten
½ cup margarine, melted

1 teaspoon salt
2 teaspoons grated lemon peel
4 to 4½ cups unbleached
white flour
2 cups blanched almonds,
slivered
½ cup powdered sugar

Dissolve yeast in warm water. Add sourdough starter. Mix in 1 cup flour. Let mixture set 12 hours or overnight to develop sponge.

raisin stollen

Stir to dissolve top crust. Add honey, eggs, margarine, salt, and lemon peel; mix well. Add 2½ cups flour to sponge; mix well.

Pour 1 cup flour on top of kneading surface. Pour sponge mixture on top of flour. Cover mixture with 1 cup flour. Knead until the flour is worked into the dough. Continue adding flour until a stiff dough has formed. Knead dough 10 minutes or until folds form in it. Place in greased bowl. Grease top of dough ball. Cover and let it rise until doubled in bulk.

Punch down dough. Knead in almonds. Divide dough into 3 equal parts. Roll the 3 dough balls into ½-inch-thick rectangles. Starting at one long end, roll a dough rectangle two turns. Next, roll remaining long end to meet first roll. Press edges together. Do this with other 2 rectangles. Place on greased cookie sheets. Cover them. Let rise until doubled in bulk.

Oil tops of stollens. Place in cold oven. Set oven at 350°F. Bake stollens 30 minutes or until done. Remove them from oven. Brush them again with oil. Sprinkle with powdered sugar. Cool them on a rack.

raisin stollen

Yield: 3 stollens

2 cups raisins
½ cup brandy
1 package active dry yeast
1 cup warm water
1 cup sourdough starter
1 cup all-purpose white flour
½ cup granulated sugar
2 eggs, beaten
½ cup margarine, melted
1 teaspoon salt
1½ teaspoons orange peel,
   grated
4 to 4½ cups all-purpose white
   flour
½ cup candied citron
1 cup blanched almonds,
   slivered
½ cup powdered sugar

Combine raisins and brandy. Let set overnight.

Dissolve yeast in warm water. Add sourdough starter. Mix in 1 cup flour. Let mixture set 12 hours or overnight to develop sponge.

Stir to dissolve crust. Add sugar, eggs, margarine, salt, and orange peel; mix well. Add 2½ cups flour to sponge; mix well.

Pour 1 cup flour on top of kneading surface. Pour sponge mixture on top of flour. Cover sponge with 1 cup flour. Knead until flour is worked into dough. Continue adding flour until a stiff dough has formed. Knead dough 10 minutes or until folds form in it. Place dough in greased bowl. Grease top. Cover bowl. Let dough rise until doubled in bulk.

Punch down dough. Knead in citron, almonds, and brandied raisins. Divide dough into 3 equal parts. Roll dough balls into ½-inch-thick rectangles. Starting at one long end, roll dough two turns. Next, roll remaining long end to meet first roll. Press edges together. Do this with other two rectangles. Place on greased cookie sheets. Cover them. Let rise until doubled in bulk.

Oil tops of stollens. Place in cold oven. Set oven at 350°F. Bake stollens 30 minutes or until done. Remove them from oven. Brush them with oil. Sprinkle with powdered sugar. Cool them on a rack.

jule kaga

Yield: 1 loaf

1 package active dry yeast
1 cup warm water
1 cup sourdough starter
1 cup unbleached white flour
¼ cup margarine, melted
½ cup granulated sugar
1 teaspoon salt
3½ to 4 cups unbleached
    white flour
1½ teaspoons ground
    cardamom
½ cup raisins
¼ cup citron, chopped
¼ cup candied cherries,
    chopped
¼ cup almonds, chopped
1 cup powdered sugar
1 tablespoon milk
¼ teaspoon vanilla
Whole nuts
Candied fruits

Dissolve yeast in warm water. Add sourdough starter. Blend thoroughly. Add 1 cup flour; mix well. Cover mixture. Let set 12 hours or overnight to develop sponge.

Stir to dissolve crust. Add margarine, sugar, and salt; mix well. Work in enough remaining flour to develop a stiff dough. Knead for 10 minutes or until dough is elastic. Place in greased bowl. Grease top of loaf. Cover it. Let rise until doubled in bulk.

Punch down dough. Knead in cardamom, raisins, citron, candied cherries, and almonds. Form dough into a round ball and place on large greased baking sheet. Cover dough. Let rise until doubled in bulk.

Bake dough ball in hot oven (400°F) for 10 minutes. Reduce heat to moderate (350°F) and continue baking for 40 minutes or until loaf is golden brown. Cool it.

Combine powdered sugar, milk, and vanilla. Frost top of loaf and decorate with nuts and candied fruits.

prune coffee kringle

Yield: 12 servings

¼ cup milk
¼ cup granulated sugar
½ teaspoon salt
2¼ cups sifted flour
¼ cup shortening
¼ cup warm water
1 package active dry yeast
½ cup sourdough starter
1 egg, beaten
1½ cups stewed prunes, pitted
    and chopped
3 tablespoons lemon juice
½ teaspoon grated lemon peel
3 tablespoons granulated sugar
1 cup powdered sugar
1 tablespoon milk
¼ teaspoon vanilla

Scald milk. Cook it to lukewarm.

Mix together ¼ cup granulated sugar, the salt, and the flour. Cut in shortening.

Pour water into large mixing bowl. Sprinkle yeast over water. Stir to dissolve yeast. Add sourdough starter. Stir in lukewarm milk. Add egg and the flour mixture. Stir until well-blended. Place mixture in greased bowl; brush top with shortening. Cover bowl. Let rise until doubled in bulk.

Meanwhile, combine prunes, lemon juice, lemon peel, and 3 tablespoons granulated sugar; mix well.

Punch down dough. Turn it out onto lightly floured board. Divide it in half. Roll out each half into an oblong about 16 × 12 inches. Place 1 oblong on large greased cookie sheet. Spread oblong with prune filling. Cover with other oblong of dough. Cover it. Let rise until doubled in bulk.

Bake oblong in preheated 350° F oven 20 minutes. Cool it.

Combine powdered sugar, milk, and vanilla; mix well. Spread this over top of cake. Cut cake into squares.

poppy treats

If you have never tasted poppy seed before, you are in for a taste treat.

Yield: 3 dozen

2 cups milk
1 package active dry yeast
½ cup sourdough starter
2 cups all-purpose white flour
½ cup shortening, melted
½ cup granulated sugar
3 egg yolks, beaten
1 teaspoon salt
3½ to 4 cups all-purpose white flour
2 12-ounce cans poppy-seed filling
1 cup walnuts, chopped fine
2 eggs, beaten

poppy treats

Scald the milk. Cool it to lukewarm.

Dissolve yeast in warm milk. Stir in sourdough starter. Mix in 2 cups flour. Let mixture stand long enough to develop a bubbly sponge.

Add shortening, sugar, egg yolks, and salt; mix well. Work in 2 cups of remaining flour. Pour 1 cup flour on top of kneading surface. Pour sponge mixture on top of flour. Cover it with 1 cup flour. Knead until flour is worked into dough. Continue adding flour until a semi-stiff dough has formed. Knead dough 10 minutes or until folds form in it. Place in greased bowl. Grease top. Cover dough. Let rise until doubled in bulk.

Punch down dough. Knead for 2 minutes. On floured surface roll out dough to ¼ inch thick. Cut into 36 3-inch square.

Combine poppy-seed filling and walnuts. Place 1 to 2 teaspoons filling in middle of each square. Fold over corners to form triangles, and pinch edges. Place on greased cookie sheet. Cover them. Let rise until doubled in bulk.

Brush triangles with beaten eggs. Place in cold oven. Set oven at 375° F. Bake triangles 15 to 20 minutes or until golden brown. Cool them on a rack.

pecan treats

Yield: 1½ dozen

3 cups unbleached white flour
1 package active dry yeast
¾ cup milk
½ cup margarine
¼ cup granulated sugar
1 teaspoon salt
1 cup sourdough starter
1 egg, beaten
½ cup honey
⅓ cup packed brown sugar
3 tablespoons margarine
1 cup pecan halves

In large mixing bowl combine 2 cups flour and the yeast. Mix until well-blended.

Scald milk. Pour it over margarine, granulated sugar, and salt. Stir until margarine melts and sugar and salt are dissolved. Cool mixture to lukewarm.

Add milk mixture and sourdough starter to flour mixture. Add egg. Beat on low speed of electric mixer 1 minute. Proceed to high speed and beat for 3 minutes. Add remaining flour. Set mixer on medium speed. Beat 3 minutes more or until batter is smooth. Cover mixing bowl and put in warm place until dough has doubled in bulk.

While dough is rising, mix honey, brown sugar, and 3 tablespoons margarine. Heat thoroughly. Divide mixture evenly among 18 greased muffin tins. Top syrup mixture with pecan halves.

Stir down dough by hand. Beat thoroughly. Drop batter by heaping tablespoons into filled greased muffin tins. Let batter rise in warm place until doubled in bulk.

Place rolls in cold oven. Set oven at 375° F and bake rolls 25 minutes or until done. Immediately invert pans to remove rolls.

raisin rolls

raisin rolls

Yield: 1 dozen

½ cup milk
¼ cup butter
1 box hot-roll mix
3 tablespoons granulated sugar
1 teaspoon grated lemon rind
½ teaspoon almond extract
½ cup sourdough starter

1 egg, beaten
¼ cup butter, melted
½ cup raisins
½ cup citron
½ cup walnuts, chopped
½ cup granulated sugar

Heat milk and ¼ cup butter to lukewarm. Dissolve yeast from hot-roll mix in warm liquid. Stir in 3 tablespoons sugar, lemon rind, almond extract, sourdough starter, and egg. Add the flour from the mix; blend well. Cover mixture and let rise in warm place until doubled in bulk.

Punch down dough. Knead until dough is no longer sticky. Roll dough to ½ inch thick. Spread ¼ cup melted butter over surface.

Combine raisins, citron, walnuts, and ½ cup sugar. Sprinkle this over butter. Roll up dough in jelly-roll fashion. Cut it into 12 equal parts. Place on greased cookie sheet. Cover them. Let rise until doubled in bulk.

Place rolls in cold oven. Set oven at 375° F. Bake rolls 15 to 20 minutes or until done. Glaze with Lemon Glaze while still warm.

lemon glaze

Yield: Glaze for 12 rolls

2 cups powdered sugar (½ box)	**3 tablespoons milk**
1 tablespoon cornstarch	**2 tablespoons lemon juice**

Combine sugar and cornstarch in medium-size mixing bowl. Blend in milk. Add lemon juice. Blend until smooth. Spread glaze over warm rolls.

cinnamon and walnut crisps

Yield: 1 dozen

1 package active dry yeast	**1 egg, beaten**
1 cup warm water	**3¼ to 3¾ cups all-purpose**
1 cup sourdough starter	**white flour**
1 cup all-purpose white flour	**1 cup brown sugar, packed**
¾ cup margarine, melted	**½ teaspoon cinnamon**
1¼ cups granulated sugar	**1 cup walnuts, chopped**
1 teaspoon salt	**1 teaspoon cinnamon**

Dissolve yeast in warm water. Add sourdough starter. Blend thoroughly. Mix in 1 cup flour. Cover mixture. Set it in warm place 12 hours or overnight.

Stir sponge to dissolve crust. Add ¼ cup margarine, ¼ cup granulated sugar, and the salt; mix well. Blend in egg. Add flour until a soft dough has formed. Pour remaining flour on kneading surface. Work flour into dough. Place dough ball in greased bowl. Grease top of dough ball. Cover it. Let rise until doubled in bulk.

Punch down dough. Knead for 2 more minutes. Roll dough into a 12 × 12-inch square. Brush dough with ¼ cup melted margarine.

Combine brown sugar, cinnamon, and remaining ¼ cup melted margarine. Spread mixture over margarine on dough. Roll dough in jelly-roll fashion. Seam edges. Cut roll into 12 equal pieces. Place on greased cookie sheet and flatten each roll with palm of your hand. Cover rolls. Let rise for 30 minutes.

Again flatten rolls with palm of your hand.

Combine 1 cup granulated sugar, the nuts, and the cinnamon. Sprinkle over rolls.

Place rolls in preheated 375° F oven 20 minutes or until golden brown on top. Remove them from pan immediately.

apricot–walnut kuchen

A challenge for the artistic baker.

Yield: 2 rings

> 1 package active dry yeast
> 1 cup warm water
> 1 cup sourdough starter
> 1 cup all-purpose white flour
> ½ cup granulated sugar
> 2 eggs, beaten
> ½ cup butter, melted
> 1 teaspoon salt
> 4 to 4½ cups all-purpose white
>   flour
> 1½ cups dried apricots
> 1 cup boiling water
> 1 cup brown sugar, packed
> ½ teaspoon cinnamon
> ½ cup walnuts, chopped

apricot–walnut kuchen

Dissolve yeast in warm water. Add sourdough starter. Mix in 1 cup flour. Let mixture set 12 hours or overnight to develop sponge.

Stir to dissolve crust. Add granulated sugar, eggs, butter, and salt; mix well. Pour 1 cup flour on top of kneading surface. Pour sponge mixture on top of flour. Cover sponge mixture with 1 cup flour. Knead until flour is worked into a dough. Continue adding flour until a stiff dough has formed. Knead dough 10 minutes or until folds form in it. Place in greased bowl. Grease top of dough. Cover it. Let rise until doubled in bulk.

Combine apricots and boiling water in a saucepan and bring to a boil. Reduce heat and simmer apricots, uncovered, about 25 minutes or until liquid is absorbed and apricots are tender. Press them through a sieve. Stir in brown sugar and cinnamon. Cool mixture.

Punch down dough. Knead for 2 minutes. Divide dough into 2 equal balls. Divide 1 ball into 2 equal parts. Roll 1 part into ½-inch-thick rectangle. Roll second part into ½-inch-thick rectangle. Spread both layers with apricot filling. Roll first rectangle loosely in jelly-roll fashion. Place this roll in the middle of second rectangle. Fold second rectangle over the rolled dough and crimp edges tightly. Place on a greased cookie sheet and form it into a semicircle. Flatten crimped edges. Next, cut dough at 1-inch intervals, cutting through only top 2 layers of dough. Repeat process with remaining dough ball. Cover them. Let rise until doubled in bulk.

Oil tops of bread. Place the rings in cold oven. Set oven at 350°F. Bake bread 40 minutes or until golden brown on top. Remove it from oven. Glaze the rings with Cream Glaze (see Index) while still warm. Decorate with walnuts.

olmitz kuchen

A traditional bread served at the Annual Church Picnic in this Kansas farming community.

Yield: 4 dozen

2 cups milk
1 package active dry yeast
½ cup sourdough starter
2 cups all-purpose white flour
½ cup shortening, melted
½ cup granulated sugar
2 eggs, beaten
1 teaspoon salt
3½ to 4 cups flour
1 cup ground poppy seeds
1 cup raisins, chopped
1 cup walnuts, chopped
¼ cup semisweet chocolate
     pieces, melted
3 tablespoons granulated sugar
2 tablespoons flour
Pinch of salt
¼ cup butter, melted

Scald milk. Cool it to lukewarm. Dissolve yeast in warm milk. Stir in sourdough starter. Mix in 2 cups flour. Let mixture stand long enough to develop a bubbly sponge. Add shortening, ½ cup sugar, the eggs, and salt; mix well. Work in 2 cups of remaining flour. Pour 1 cup flour on top of kneading surface. Pour sponge mixture on top of flour. Cover it with 1 cup flour. Knead until flour is worked into dough. Continue adding flour until a semi-stiff dough has formed. Knead dough 10 minutes or until folds form in it. Place in greased bowl. Grease top of dough. Cover it. Let rise until doubled in bulk.

While dough is rising, combine ground poppy seeds, raisins, walnuts, and melted chocolate pieces to make the filling.

Next, make the topping by combining the 3 tablespoons sugar, the flour, salt, and butter. Mix until crumbly.

Punch down dough. Knead for an additional 2 minutes. Using a teaspoon, take out pieces of dough about the size of a large walnut. Place these on floured board. Spread them flat. Place about a teaspoon of filling on dough and pinch ends together. Place smooth-side-up on greased cookie sheet. Brush tops with melted butter and sprinkle with topping. Cover dough. Let rise until doubled.

Bake at 400° F for 12 minutes or until brown.

hot cross buns

These are traditionally served on Good Friday. They also make a delicious treat for Easter morning.

Yield: 12 buns

**1 8-ounce package cream
   cheese, softened
1 egg
2 tablespoons granulated sugar
¾ cup white raisins
½ cup milk
¼ cup margarine
1 box hot-roll mix
½ cup sourdough starter
1 egg, beaten**

Blenderize cream cheese, egg, and sugar. Stir in raisins. Set mixture aside. Heat milk and margarine to lukewarm. Dissolve yeast from hot-roll mix in warm liquid. Stir in sourdough starter and beaten egg. Add flour mixture from hot-roll mix. Blend well. Cover mixture. Let rise until doubled in bulk.

Punch down dough. Knead until it is no longer sticky. Divide it into 12 equal dough balls. Roll each dough ball into a ¼-inch-thick circle. Put 1 tablespoon of cheese mixture in center of each dough circle. Bring edges together and pinch closed. Place in greased 8-inch-square pan, seamed-edge-down. Cover buns. Let rise until doubled in bulk.

Bake buns in preheated 375° F oven 20 minutes or until done.

Decorate warm buns by drizzling Cream Glaze (see Index) to resemble crosses on top of them. Serve them warm.

breakfast dishes

family pancakes

Nutritious pancakes for a family feast.

Yield: 12 pancakes

1½ cups buttermilk biscuit mix
⅓ cup wheat germ

2 eggs, beaten
½ cup sourdough starter
¾ cup milk

Combine all ingredients and mix until smooth. Using a ¼-cup measure, pour batter onto heated grill. Grill until pancakes are dry around edges and bubbles form on top. Turn; grill other side until golden brown. (For thinner pancakes, increase milk by ½ cup.)

silver-dollar pancakes

silver-dollar pancakes

Yield: 2 dozen

2 eggs, beaten
1 cup milk
¼ cup butter, melted
½ cup sourdough starter
1 tablespoon sugar
2 cups self-rising flour

Combine liquid ingredients and sugar in large bowl. Add self-rising flour; mix until smooth. Pour mixture 1 tablespoon at a time on preheated grill. Grill it until bubbles form; turn and bake remaining side until golden brown. Serve them warm. (If batter is too thick, add more milk.)

apple-butter stacks

A delicious blend of apple butter and sour cream sandwiched between sourdough pancakes.

Yield: 4 stacks

1½ cups buttermilk biscuit mix
⅓ cup wheat germ
2 eggs, beaten
½ cup sourdough starter

¾ cup milk
1 cup apple butter
½ cup sour cream

Combine biscuit mix, wheat germ, eggs, sourdough starter, and milk. Mix until smooth. Using a ¼-cup measure, pour batter onto heated grill. Grill pancakes until dry around edges and bubbles form on top. Turn; grill other side until golden brown. Spread sour cream on pancakes; top with apple butter; stack them.

apricot-filled pancakes

Yield: 12 pancakes

3 eggs, beaten
½ cup milk
½ cup sourdough starter
6 teaspoons butter
½ cup pancake mix
¾ cup apricot preserves
1 cup powdered sugar
1 cup English walnuts, ground

Combine eggs, milk, and sourdough starter. Add pancake mix and stir until smooth.

For each pancake place ½ teaspoon butter in 6- or 7-inch skillet; heat it until bubbly. Pour in 2 tablespoons batter and roll pan until bottom is coated. Cook batter until underside is brown. Turn and brown other side. Cook remaining pancakes in the same manner. Keep them hot on baking sheet in warm oven until ready to fill. Place 1 tablespoon preserves in middle of each pancake. Roll them up. Arrange them on serving plate and sprinkle with powdered sugar and ground nuts.

apricot-filled pancakes

sourdough oatmeal stacks

sourdough oatmeal stacks

Yield: 12 pancakes

1½ cups uncooked oatmeal	2 teaspoons baking powder
2 cups sourdough starter	1 teaspoon salt
1 cup all-purpose white flour	2 eggs, beaten
1 cup milk	¼ cup margarine, melted
2 tablespoons brown sugar	½ cup granulated sugar
1 teaspoon baking soda	

Combine oatmeal, sourdough starter, flour, and milk. Let mixture set overnight in warm place.

Next morning add brown sugar, baking soda, baking powder, salt, eggs, and margarine to oatmeal mixture; mix well. If mixture is too dry, add more milk. If too moist, add more flour. Using a ½-cup measure, pour batter onto hot grill. Cook about 2½ minutes on each side. Stack pancakes, sprinkling granulated sugar between each layer. Serve them warm.

early-riser pancakes

This is a delicious and nutritious way to start the day.

Yield: 6 to 8 pancakes

⅓ cup milk
1 cup biscuit mix

½ cup sourdough starter
1 egg, beaten

Combine all ingredients and mix until smooth. Using a ¼-cup measure, pour batter onto heated grill. Grill until pancakes are dry around edges and bubbles form on top. Turn; grill other side until golden brown. (For thinner pancakes, increase milk by ¼ cup.) Serve with melted butter and warm maple syrup.

blueberry griddle cakes

blueberry griddle cakes

Yield: 6 to 8 servings

2 cups all-purpose white flour
1½ teaspoons baking soda
½ teaspoon salt
1 tablespoon granulated sugar
1 egg, beaten
1½ cups milk
1 cup sourdough starter
1½ tablespoons oil
3 cups fresh blueberries
1 cup granulated sugar

Mix dry ingredients, except 1 cup granulated sugar. Combine liquid ingredients and add mixture to dry ingredients. Beat until batter is free from lumps. Using a ½-cup measure, pour batter onto preheated grill. When pancakes are puffed and full of bubbles, turn them and brown other side. Turn only once. Form stacks by alternating a pancake layer with blueberries sprinkled with granulated sugar. Place in warm oven to maintain heat. Serve with warm blueberry syrup, prepared by mixing blueberries with 1 cup sugar.

orange treats

Yield: 6 servings

2 eggs, beaten
¼ cup milk
1 tablespoon sugar
1 teaspoon dried orange peel
¼ cup orange juice

6 slices sourdough
   Whole-Wheat Molasses
   Bread (see Index)
Oil for frying

Combine eggs, milk, sugar, orange peel, and juice. Mix well. Dip bread slices in egg mixture, lightly coating both sides.

Heat frying oil in skillet and brown the bread on both sides. Serve at once with warm syrup.

whole-wheat english muffins

Yield: 18 muffins

1 package active dry yeast
2 cups warm water
½ cup sourdough starter
2 cups all-purpose white flour
2 tablespoons margarine,
   melted

3 tablespoons honey
1 teaspoon salt
2 cups whole-wheat flour
1½ to 2 cups all-purpose white
   flour
½ cup cornmeal

Dissolve yeast in warm water. Add sourdough starter. Blend thoroughly. Mix in 2 cups flour. Cover mixture. Set it in warm place 12 hours or overnight to develop sourdough.

Next morning stir down sponge. Add margarine, honey, and salt to sponge; mix well. Add whole-wheat flour and enough white flour to form a stiff dough.

Turn out dough onto floured board; knead about 2 minutes or until dough is manageable and can be formed into a ball. (Dough may be slightly sticky.) Place in greased bowl, turning to grease top. Cover dough and let rise in warm place, free from draft, until doubled in bulk — about 1 hour.

Punch down dough; divide it in half. On a board heavily sprinkled with cornmeal, pat each dough half to ½ inch thick. Cut dough into circles, using a 3-inch-diameter cutter. Place the circles about 2 inches apart on waxed paper. Cover them and let rise in warm place until doubled in bulk.

Place the circles on lightly greased medium-hot griddle or skillet (a drop of water will sizzle), cornmeal-side-down. Bake them until well-browned, about 10 minutes on each side. Cool them. Store in plastic bag.

waffles

Yield: Eight 4-inch squares

1 cup biscuit mix	1 egg, beaten
½ cup sourdough starter	1 tablespoon oil
½ cup milk	

Combine all ingredients; mix well. Pour half of mixture on preheated waffle grill. Bake batter until golden brown. Bake remaining batter in same manner. Serve with melted butter and warm syrup.

ham and cheese toast

A quick and nutritious busy-morning breakfast.

Yield: 4 sandwiches

8 slices Sourdough White Bread (see Index)	8 ounces chopped ham
Butter to taste	8 ounces shredded Swiss cheese

Toast bread. Spread with butter. Top 4 slices of toast with ham. Sprinkle shredded cheese over ham. Place under broiler to melt cheese. Top with remaining slices of buttered toast. Serve them warm.

banana wheat french toast

Yield: 6 servings

1 loaf Banana Wheat Bread (see Index)	½ cup milk
4 eggs, beaten	1 teaspoon cinnamon
	Oil for frying

Slice bread into 12 thick slices.

Combine eggs, milk, and cinnamon. Soak each bread slice in egg mixture. Fry bread slices in hot skillet just long enough to brown both sides. Serve toast warm with butter and maple syrup.

Pictured on next two pages:
1) salami tartare
2) pizza toast
3) ham and cheese toast
4) canadian treat
5) breakfast supreme

raisin english muffins

A delicious addition to a Sunday brunch.

Yield: 18 muffins

1 package active dry yeast
2 cups warm water
½ cup sourdough starter
2 cups all-purpose white flour
2 tablespoons shortening,
melted
2 tablespoons molasses
1 teaspoon salt
½ cup raisins
3½ to 4 cups all-purpose white
flour
½ cup cornmeal

Dissolve yeast in warm water. Add sourdough starter. Blend thoroughly. Mix in 2 cups flour. Cover mixture. Set it in warm place 12 hours or overnight to develop sourdough.

Next morning stir down sponge. Add shortening, molasses, salt, and raisins to sponge; mix well. Add flour until a stiff dough has formed.

Turn it out onto floured board; knead about 2 minutes, or until dough is manageable and can be formed into a ball. (Dough may be slightly sticky.) Place in greased bowl, turning it to grease top. Cover dough and let rise in warm place, free from draft, until doubled in bulk — about 1 hour.

Punch down dough; divide it in half. On a board heavily sprinkled with cornmeal, pat each dough half to ½ inch thick. Cut into circles, using a 3-inch-diameter cutter. Place the circles about 2 inches apart on waxed paper. Cover and let them rise in warm place until doubled in bulk.

Place the circles on lightly greased medium-hot griddle or skillet (a drop of water will sizzle). Bake them until well-browned, about 10 minutes on each side. Cool them. Store in plastic bag.

sticky buns

Yield: 1½ dozen

¼ cup warm water
1 cup sourdough starter
½ cup milk
¼ margarine
¾ cup granulated sugar
3¼ to 3½ cups all-purpose
    white flour
¼ teaspoon salt
1 egg, beaten

brown-sugar syrup

½ cup water
¼ cup margarine
1¼ cups brown sugar

filling

¼ cup margarine
¼ cup granulated sugar
1 teaspoon allspice
½ cup currants

Dissolve yeast in warm water. Set yeast mixture in warm place for 10 minutes or until mixture doubles in volume. Add sourdough starter.

Scald milk.

Combine ¼ cup margarine and ¼ cup granulated sugar. Pour scalded milk over margarine mixture. Stir to dissolve sugar. Cool it to lukewarm. Add to yeast mixture.

Combine flour and salt. Make a well in center of flour mixture and pour milk mixture and egg into it. Work flour into the liquid until it forms a medium-stiff dough.

Place dough on floured surface and knead 10 minutes or until dough is elastic. Shape it into a dough ball and place in greased bowl. Grease top. Cover dough. Let rise until doubled in bulk.

While dough is rising, combine syrup ingredients in small, heavy saucepan. Stir until sugar dissolves, and bring mixture to rapid boil. Reduce heat to moderate and continue cooking syrup for 10 minutes or until it has consistency and color of maple syrup. Cool it to lukewarm.

Punch down dough. Place on lightly floured surface and knead for 2 minutes. Roll dough into a 12 × 12-inch square.

Brush dough with ¼ cup melted butter from filling ingredients. Combine sugar and allspice. Sprinkle sugar mixture evenly over dough. Spread currants evenly over this.

Dribble half the brown-sugar syrup over currants. With your hands roll dough into a tight cylinder. Cut cylinder crosswise into 1-inch rounds.

Pour remaining syrup into greased 10-inch-round cake pan. Arrange rounds, cut-side-down, in a circle around edge of pan. Continue this pattern with remaining rounds until pan is full. Let rise 30 minutes or until doubled in bulk.

Preheat oven to 350° F. Bake buns 30 minutes or until golden brown. Remove them from oven and invert them onto a rack. Serve them warm.

baked chocolate-chip doughnuts

Baking doughnuts reduces their caloric content.

Yield: 2½ dozen

2 cups milk	4 egg yolks, beaten
1 package active dry yeast	1 teaspoon salt
½ cup sourdough starter	3½ to 4 cups all-purpose white
2 cups all-purpose white flour	flour
1 cup butter, melted	1 6-ounce package chocolate
½ cup granulated sugar	chips

Scald milk. Cool it to lukewarm. Dissolve yeast in warm milk. Stir in sourdough starter. Mix in 2 cups flour. Let mixture stand long enough to develop a bubbly sponge.

Add ½ cup butter, the sugar, egg yolks, and salt; mix well. Work in 2 cups of remaining flour.

Pour 1 cup flour on top of kneading surface. Pour sponge mixture on top of flour. Cover this with 1 cup flour. Knead until flour is worked into dough. Continue adding flour until a semi-stiff dough has formed. Knead dough 10 minutes or until folds form in it. Place in greased bowl. Grease top. Cover dough. Let rise until doubled in bulk.

Punch down dough. Knead for 2 minutes. Turn out dough onto floured surface and roll it to ½ inch thick. Cut it into 2½-inch rounds with a doughnut cutter. Place rounds 2 inches apart on greased baking sheet and brush them with ¼ cup melted butter. Let rise in warm place for 20 to 30 minutes.

Bake doughnuts at 425° F for 8 to 10 minutes. Brush with ¼ cup butter, then cool them enough to handle.

Dip tops of warm doughnuts into Clear Glaze. Place on racks, tops up, to cool.

clear glaze

Yield: Glaze for 3- to 4-dozen doughnuts

4 cups powdered sugar
2 tablespoons cornstarch
¼ cup milk
1 teaspoon vanilla

Combine powdered sugar and cornstarch in medium-size bowl. Add milk and vanilla. Blend until smooth.

yankee doodle snipdoodle

An English tea cake with an American addition of delicious sourdough flavoring.

Yield: One 8 × 12-inch cake

1 cup margarine	4 teaspoons baking powder
1 cup granulated sugar	½ teaspoon salt
½ cup brown sugar, packed	1 cup sourdough starter
2 eggs	½ cup milk
2 cups all-purpose white flour	¼ cup granulated sugar
⅓ cup whole-wheat flour	1 teaspoon cinnamon

Cream margarine and ½ cup granulated sugar and the brown sugar until light and fluffy. Beat in eggs, 1 at a time.

Combine white and whole-wheat flours, baking powder, and salt.

Combine starter and milk. Add dry mixture and starter mixture alternately until all ingredients are blended into the batter.

Lightly grease and flour an 8 × 12-inch cake pan. Pour cake batter into greased pan.

Combine ¼ cup sugar and the cinnamon; sprinkle over top of batter. Place pan in middle of 350° F oven and bake cake 50 minutes or until a toothpick inserted in center comes out clean. Serve it warm.

canadian treat

Yield: 4 open-faced sandwiches

4 slices sourdough Caraway Rye Loaf (see Index)	8 slices Canadian bacon
¼ cup butter	4 ounces mozzarella cheese, grated
1 small onion, sliced crosswise	4 apple rings
1 green pepper, sliced into strips	1 bunch watercress
1 teaspoon freshly ground black pepper	

Toast the bread. Melt butter in cast-iron skillet. Divide onion slices into rings. Sauté onions and green pepper in butter until soft. Divide vegetables evenly among toasted bread. Sprinkle with pepper. Top vegetables with 2 slices Canadian bacon per toast slice. Sprinkle bacon with cheese. Place slices under broiler until cheese melts. Garnish with apple rings and watercress.

camping bacon and eggs

Yield: 4 servings

8 slices sourdough
  Whole-Wheat Molasses
  Bread (see Index)
2 tablespoons butter, softened
4 hard-cooked eggs, sliced
  diagonally
1 teaspoon salt
¼ teaspoon white pepper
4 slices bacon, cut in half
  crosswise

Spread each bread slice with butter. Arrange sliced eggs on half of bread slices. Sprinkle with salt and pepper. Top with remaining bread slices, butter-side-down.

Place sandwiches in long-handled, hinged wire broiler or toaster and top each with 2 half-slices bacon, side by side. Brown both sides of sandwiches over hot coals, leaving the side with bacon until last. Serve them hot.

hole-in-one eggs

A cast-iron skillet gives this breakfast treat a distinctive taste all its own.

Yield: 6 servings

Oil for frying
6 1-inch-thick slices
  Sourdough White Bread
  (see Index)
1 teaspoon salt
¼ teaspoon pepper
6 eggs

Pour frying oil into skillet. Heat thoroughly.

Cut centers from bread slices, using a doughnut cutter. (Use centers for making croutons.) Place prepared bread in heated skillet.

Break an egg. Pour it in the center of a bread slice. Fry bread until browned and egg white is cooked. Turn the bread and egg at same time. Fry remaining side to desired doneness.

Prepare remaining servings in same manner. Replenish oil in skillet as needed. Remember to preheat oil each time before frying bread.

breakfast supreme

Yield: 4 open-faced sandwiches

4 slices sourdough Caraway
Rye Loaf (see Index)
Butter as needed
8 ounces cooked ham, sliced
thick
2 tomatoes, sliced crosswise
1 teaspoon freshly ground
pepper

4 ounces Muenster cheese,
sliced
4 ounces dried beef, sliced
thin
4 eggs
1 tablespoon chopped chives

Toast the bread. Spread toast with butter. Top with ham slices. Arrange tomato slices on top of ham. Sprinkle with pepper.

Cut cheese slices in half diagonally. Arrange over tomatoes. Place sandwiches under broiler to soften cheese. (Do not let it melt.) Top cheese with dried beef.

Fry eggs sunny-side-up. Drain grease. Trim eggs so that white does not hang over sandwich edges. Place trimmed eggs on top of beef slices. Garnish with chives.

creamed-ground-beef baskets

An Army breakfast tradition.

Yield: 6 servings

1 tablespoon butter
1 cup flour
1 cup milk
½ teaspoon salt
½ teaspoon pepper
½ pound ground beef
1 loaf sourdough white bread
½ cup butter, melted

Melt 1 tablespoon butter in small saucepan. Remove from heat and add flour, stirring with wire whisk. Add milk gradually, stirring mixture constantly until sauce has thickened. Stir in salt and pepper.

Brown the ground beef and add to white sauce; mix well.

Trim crusts from bread. Cut bread into blocks, leaving a cavity in centers. Brush bread baskets with melted butter. Place on a cookie sheet and toast them under broiler until light golden brown. Pour creamed ground beef over toast baskets. Serve immediately.

muffins and quick breads

hazelnut kuchen

Yield: One 9-inch loaf

    1 cup whole-wheat flour
    1½ cups all-purpose white
        flour
    1 teaspoon salt
    1 teaspoon baking soda
    1 cup honey
    ¼ cup butter
    1 egg, beaten
    ⅔ cup milk
    ½ cup sourdough starter
    1 cup hazelnuts, chopped
    1 6-ounce package semisweet
        chocolate chips

hazelnut kuchen

Sift dry ingredients.

Cream honey and butter. Combine milk and sourdough starter. Add dry ingredients alternately with sourdough-starter mixture to honey butter. Stir in nuts.

Pour batter into greased 9-inch loaf pan. Bake mixture at 300° F for 1 hour and 40 minutes or until done. Remove loaf from pan to cool. Melt chocolate chips. Coat top of loaf with melted chocolate.

yam bread

Yield: Two 9-inch loaves

1 cup margarine
2 cups granulated sugar
¾ cup brown sugar
3 eggs, beaten
2 teaspoons cinnamon
1 teaspoon ground cloves
1 teaspoon nutmeg
1 teaspoon salt
⅓ cup water

½ cup sourdough starter
2 cups yams, mashed
3¼ cups all-purpose white
  flour
1 teaspoon baking soda
2 teaspoons baking powder
1 teaspoon vanilla
1 cup walnuts, chopped

Cream margarine and white and brown sugar; add eggs, cinnamon, cloves, nutmeg, and salt.

Combine sourdough starter, water, and yams. Mix together flour, baking soda, and baking powder. Alternately add dry ingredients and sourdough mixture to margarine mixture. Add vanilla and walnuts.

Turn batter into 2 greased 9-inch loaf pans. Bake loaves at 325° F for 70 minutes or until done. Cool them 10 minutes before removing from pans.

whole-wheat oatmeal bread

A combination of oatmeal and whole wheat gives this bread an unusual flavor.

Yield: One 9 × 5-inch loaf

1 cup whole-wheat flour
1 cup unbleached white flour
½ cup old-fashioned oats,
  uncooked
½ cup brown sugar, packed
1 teaspoon cinnamon
1 tablespoon baking powder

1 teaspoon soda
½ teaspoon salt
⅓ cup milk
1 cup sourdough starter
⅓ cup liquid margarine
1 egg, beaten
½ cup raisins (optional)

Combine dry ingredients; add milk, sourdough starter, liquid margarine, and beaten egg, mixing just until moistened. Stir in raisins.

Grease and flour a 9 × 5-inch loaf pan. Spoon bread dough into pan. Bake at 350° F for 50 minutes or until done. Cool the bread. Remove it from pan.

nut oatmeal bread

The touch of mace in this bread adds a taste sensation to a brunch.

Yield: One 9 × 5-inch loaf

2 cups all-purpose white flour
½ cup old-fashioned oats,
    uncooked
½ cup granulated sugar
½ teaspoon mace
1 tablespoon baking powder
1 teaspoon soda
½ teaspoon salt
½ cup nuts
⅓ cup milk
1 cup sourdough starter
⅓ cup oil
1 egg, beaten

Combine dry ingredients and nuts. Add milk, sourdough starter, oil, and beaten egg, mixing just until moistened.

Grease and flour a 9 × 5-inch loaf pan. Spoon bread dough into pan. Bake it at 350° F for 50 minutes or until done. Cool the bread. Remove it from pan.

banana bread

Yield: One 9-inch loaf

1½ cups all-purpose flour
½ teaspoon baking soda
½ teaspoon baking powder
¼ teaspoon salt
¼ teaspoon orange peel,
    grated

½ cup margarine
1 cup granulated sugar
2 eggs, beaten
1 teaspoon vanilla
¾ cup bananas, mashed
½ cup sourdough starter

Sift together flour, baking soda, baking powder, and salt. Add orange peel. Cream margarine and sugar until fluffy. Add eggs; beat until well-blended.

Combine vanilla, bananas, and sourdough starter. Add this mixture alternately with dry ingredients to creamed margarine and sugar.

Pour batter into greased and floured 9-inch loaf pan and bake it in preheated 350° F oven 1 hour or until done. Remove loaf from pan and cool it.

bran date bread

bran date bread

Yield: 3 small loaves

2 teaspoons baking soda	**1½ cups all-purpose white**
1 8-ounce package dates, cut up	**flour**
1⅔ cups boiling water	**1 cup whole-wheat flour**
1 cup margarine	**½ cup unprocessed wheat**
2 cups granulated sugar	**bran**
2 eggs, beaten	**⅓ cup wheat germ**
½ cup sourdough starter	**2 cups almonds, sliced**

Mix baking soda and dates. Pour boiling water over dates and let stand until cool.

Cream margarine and sugar. Add eggs and beat until smooth.

Combine sourdough starter and date mixture.

Combine flour, wheat bran, and wheat germ. To creamed mixture add alternately dates and flour mixture, mixing well after each addition. Fold in nuts.

Pour batter into well-greased and floured small loaf pans. Bake batter at 375° F for 10 minutes, then lower temperature to 350° F and bake 50 minutes more or until done. Remove bread from oven. Let stand 10 minutes before removing from pans.

75

danish heart loaf

danish heart loaf

A treat for a low-cholesterol diet.

Yield: One 9-inch loaf

¾ cup brown sugar
2 cups all-purpose white flour
1 teaspoon baking soda
1 tablespoon baking powder
2 teaspoons apple-pie spice
½ teaspoon salt

½ cup sourdough starter
½ cup skim milk
1½ ounces liquid egg
    substitute
¼ cup honey

Mix dry ingredients

Combine sourdough starter, milk, egg substitute, and honey. Add liquid mixture to dry ingredients. Blend well.

Pour mixture into greased 9-inch loaf pan. Bake it at 350° F for 60 minutes or until done. Remove loaf from pan to cool.

christmas fruit loaf

An unusual blend of bananas, raisins, and candied fruit.

Yield: One 9-inch loaf

christmas fruit loaf

1½ cups unbleached white flour
½ teaspoon baking soda
½ teaspoon baking powder
¼ teaspoon salt
½ cup butter
1 cup granulated sugar
2 eggs, beaten
1 teaspoon vanilla
¾ cup bananas, mashed
½ cup sourdough starter
½ cup raisins
½ cup candied fruit
3 ounces cream cheese
½ cup margarine
1 teaspoon vanilla
½ box powdered sugar
1 cup almonds, slivered
3 red candied cherries
3 green candied cherries

Sift together flour, baking soda, baking powder, and salt.

Cream butter and sugar until fluffy. Add eggs; beat until well-blended.

Combine vanilla, bananas, and sourdough starter. Add to egg mixture alternately with dry ingredients. Fold in raisins and candied fruit. Pour mixture into greased and floured 9-inch loaf pan. Bake loaf at 350° F for 60 minutes or until done. Remove it from pan to cool.

While cake is cooling, combine cream cheese, ¼ cup margarine, the vanilla, and powdered sugar. Mix until smooth. Spread cooled loaf with this frosting. Decorate with almonds and cherries, as shown.

austrian honey loaf

Yield: One 9-inch loaf

**2½ cups unbleached white
flour
1 teaspoon baking soda
1 teaspoon salt
3 tablespoons margarine
1 cup clover honey
1 egg, beaten
⅔ cup milk
½ cup sourdough starter**

Sift dry ingredients together.
Cream margarine and honey.
Combine milk and sourdough starter. Add dry ingredients alternately with sourdough-starter mixture to honey butter.
Pour batter into greased 9-inch loaf pan. Bake loaf at 300° F for 1 hour and 40 minutes. Cool it on a rack.

tropical-isle coffee cake

Yield: One 8-inch cake

**½ cup shortening
¾ cup brown sugar
1 egg, beaten
¼ cup water
⅓ cup sourdough starter
1½ cups unbleached white
flour
½ cup whole-wheat flour**

**3 tablespoons nonfat dry milk
2 teaspoons baking powder
½ teaspoon salt
1 cup fresh coconut, grated
1 teaspoon cinnamon
½ cup brown sugar
¼ cup evaporated milk**

Cream shortening and ¾ cup brown sugar. Beat in egg, milk, water, and sourdough starter.
Combine flours, dry milk, baking powder, and salt. Add to sugar mixture. Mix well. Pour batter into greased 8 × 8 × 2-inch pan.
Combine coconut, cinnamon, ½ cup brown sugar, and evaporated milk. Spread on top of batter. Bake cake in 350° F oven 30 minutes or until done. Serve it warm.

cherry-berry coffee cake

cherry-berry coffee cake

Yield: One 8-inch-round cake

½ cup margarine
¾ cup sugar
1 egg, beaten
¼ cup milk
⅓ cup sourdough starter
2 cups all-purpose flour
2 teaspoons baking powder
½ teaspoon salt
1 No. 2 can cherry pie filling

Cream margarine and sugar. Add egg; mix well. Blend in milk and sourdough starter.

Combine dry ingredients. Add to margarine mixture.

Spread half of batter in greased 8-inch-round container; cover with ¾ can pie filling. Spread with remaining batter; top with remaining filling. Bake cake in 375° F oven 30 minutes or until done.

cinnamon–pecan coffee cake

Yield: One 8-inch cake

¾ cup butter
¾ cup granulated sugar
1 egg, beaten
2 cups all-purpose white flour
2 teaspoons baking powder
½ teaspoon salt
1 teaspoon cinnamon
¼ cup milk
⅓ cup sourdough starter

topping

1 cup brown sugar
¼ teaspoon salt
3 tablespoons flour
2 cups pecans, chopped

Cream ½ cup butter and the sugar. Beat in egg.

Combine flour, baking powder, salt, and cinnamon. Add to creamed mixture alternately with milk and sourdough starter. Pour batter into greased 8 × 8 × 2-inch pan.

Combine topping ingredients. Sprinkle over batter. Bake cake in 350° F oven for 35 minutes or until done.

plain muffins

Yield: 1½ dozen

2 cups all-purpose white flour
¼ cup granulated sugar
1 tablespoon baking powder
½ teaspoon baking soda
½ teaspoon salt
1 cup milk
½ cup sourdough starter
⅓ cup salad oil
1 egg, beaten

Combine flour, sugar, baking powder, baking soda, and salt in large bowl.

Combine milk, sourdough starter, oil, and beaten egg.

Make a well in center of flour mixture. Pour the liquid into the well. Stir just enough to moisten flour. *Do not beat.*

Pour about ¼ cup batter into 18 well-greased muffin tins. Bake muffins in preheated 400° F oven 20 to 25 minutes or until golden brown. Remove them from tins to cool.

whole-wheat cinnamon muffins

Yield: 1½ dozen

> ¼ cup brown sugar, packed
> 1 cup all-purpose white flour
> 1 cup whole-wheat flour
> 1 tablespoon baking powder
> ½ teaspoon baking soda
> 1 teaspoon cinnamon
> ½ teaspoon salt
> 1 cup milk
> ½ cup sourdough starter
> ⅓ cup salad oil
> 1 egg, beaten

Combine sugar, flours, baking powder, baking soda, cinnamon, and salt in large bowl.

Combine milk, sourdough starter, oil, and beaten egg.

Make a well in center of flour mixture. Pour the liquid into the well. Stir just enough to moisten flour. *Do not beat.*

Pour about ½ cup batter into well-greased muffin tins. Bake muffins in preheated 400° F oven 20 to 25 minutes or until golden brown. Remove them from tins to cool.

easy corn muffins

An added flavor treat to a muffin mix.

Yield: 9 muffins

> 1 7½-ounce corn-muffin mix
> ½ cup warm water
> ½ cup sourdough starter

Combine muffin mix and warm water; mix until smooth. Stir in sourdough starter. Pour mixture into 9 greased muffin tins. Bake muffins in preheated 400°F oven 15 to 20 minutes. Remove muffins from pan immediately.

grape-jelly muffins

Yield: 1½ dozen

    2 cups all-purpose white flour
    ¼ cup granulated sugar
    1 tablespoon baking powder
    ½ teaspoon baking soda
    ½ teaspoon salt
    1 cup milk
    ¼ cup sourdough starter
    ⅓ cup salad oil
    1 egg, beaten
    ¾ cup grape jelly

Combine flour, sugar, baking powder, baking soda, and salt in large bowl.

Combine milk, sourdough starter, oil, and beaten egg.

Make a well in center of flour mixture. Pour the liquid into the well. Stir just enough to moisten flour. *Do not beat.*

Pour about 2 tablespoons batter into each of 18 well-greased muffin tins. Spoon 1 teaspoon jelly on top of batter. Cover jelly with 2 more tablespoons batter.

Bake muffins in preheated 400°F oven 20 to 25 minutes or until golden brown. Remove from tins to cool.

cheesy corn muffins

Yield: 9 muffins

    1 7½-ounce corn-muffin mix
    ½ cup warm water
    ½ cup sourdough starter
    ½ cup cheddar cheese, grated

Combine muffin mix and water; mix until smooth. Stir in sourdough starter. Fold in cheese.

Pour mixture into 9 greased muffin tins. Bake muffins in preheated 450°F oven 15 to 20 minutes. Remove muffins from pan immediately.

honey buns

Yield: 12 muffin cakes

> **2 cups all-purpose white flour**
> **¾ cup brown sugar**
> **1 tablespoon baking powder**
> **1 teaspoon baking soda**
> **2 teaspoons cinnamon**
> **¼ teaspoon nutmeg**
> **½ teaspoon salt**
> **½ cup sourdough starter**
> **½ cup skim milk**
> **1 egg, beaten**
> **¼ cup honey**

Combine dry ingredients in mixing bowl.

Combine sourdough starter, milk, egg, and honey. Add liquid mixture to dry ingredients; blend well.

Spoon mixture into 12 greased muffin tins. Bake cakes at 350° F for 20 to 25 minutes or until done. Remove them from muffin tins. Serve them warm.

walnut muffins

Yield: 12 muffins

> **1½ cups all-purpose flour**
> **¼ cup wheat germ**
> **2 teaspoons baking powder**
> **½ teaspoon salt**
> **½ cup granulated sugar**
> **1 egg, beaten**
> **½ cup milk**
> **½ cup sourdough starter**
> **¼ cup butter, melted**
> **½ cup walnuts, chopped**
> **coarsely**

Stir flour, wheat germ, baking powder, salt, and sugar together.

Combine egg, milk, and sourdough starter. Stir in butter. Add this to flour mixture. Stir just until dry ingredients are moistened. Stir in walnuts.

Drop batter into 12 greased muffin tins. Bake muffins at 375° F until tops are lightly browned — 20 to 25 minutes.

main dishes and dressings

sourdough beirocks (modern version)

Yield: 6 servings

1 small head cabbage, shredded
½ cup coarsely chopped onions
1 teaspoon salt
¼ teaspoon pepper
½ cup water
½ pound ground beef
1 box hot-roll mix
1 cup warm water
1 egg, beaten
1 package sour-cream-sauce mix (1.25 ounces)

sourdough beirocks

Combine cabbage, onions, salt, pepper, and water in skillet. Cover skillet and simmer vegetables until cabbage is tender. Stir occasionally.

Brown the ground beef. Drain it.

Combine cabbage-and-onion mixture with beef.

Dissolve yeast from hot-roll mix in warm water as directed on package. Add beaten egg; blend well.

Combine sour-cream-sauce mix with flour from hot-roll mix. Add flour mixture to yeast mixture; blend well. Cover and let rise in warm place until doubled in bulk (about 45 minutes).

Punch down dough and place on well-floured surface. Roll out dough to a 16 × 20-inch rectangle. Cut it into 4-inch squares. Fill each square with a heaping tablespoon of cabbage–beef mixture; bring corners together. Pinch edges together.

Turn them pinched-side-down on greased cookie sheet and bake about 30 minutes at 350° F.

hamburger towers

Yield: 8 servings

½ cup mayonnaise
½ teaspoon celery salt
1 loaf Coffee-Can Cheese
　　Bread (see Index)
8 hamburger patties, fried
8 slices tomato

8 slices onion
8 slices cucumber
4 hard-cooked eggs, halved
　　crosswise
8 olives

Combine mayonnaise and celery salt.

Slice bread into 8 thick slices; toast it. Spread mayonnaise evenly over toasted bread. Place a hamburger patty on each slice of bread. Top each with a tomato slice, onion slice, cucumber slice, hard-cooked egg half, and an olive. Secure the tower with wooden skewers.

polish-sausage rolls

polish-sausage rolls

Add variety to your next outdoor picnic with these.

Yield: 8 servings

½ recipe Crescent Rolls (see
　　Index)

8 Polish sausages
1 egg, beaten

Prepare sourdough Crescent Roll dough. Let rise. Divide dough into 2 equal parts. Use one half of dough for bread. Divide remaining dough into 2 equal parts. Roll each part into a ¼-inch-thick circle. Cut each circle into 4 equal parts. Roll Polish sausages in dough. Place on greased cookie sheet. Cover them. Let rise 30 minutes.

Brush rolls with beaten egg. Bake them in preheated 375° F oven 20 minutes or until dough is golden brown. Serve immediately.

hot dogs american-style

hot dogs american-style

A different version of Pigs in the Blanket.

Yield: 8 servings

**½ recipe Sourdough White
    Bread (see Index)**
8 all-beef hot dogs
½ cup catsup
**8 ounces mozzarella cheese,
    shredded**
½ cup fried bacon crumbs

Prepare sourdough bread. Let rise. Divide dough in half. Use one half for a small loaf of bread. Roll remaining half of dough into a ½-inch-thick rectangle. Cut it into 8 equal pieces. Wrap each hot dog in dough. Place on greased cookie sheet. Let rise for 30 minutes.

Bake them in preheated 375° F oven 20 minutes or until rolls are golden brown. Remove them from oven.

Split rolls and pull hot dogs from buns so that one end is exposed, as illustrated. Pour 1 tablespoon catsup in each split bun. Top catsup with 1 ounce shredded cheese. Return hot dogs to oven. Continue baking until cheese has melted. Remove them from oven. Garnish with bacon crumbs. Serve at once.

texas toast sandwich

texas toast sandwich

Yield: 6 servings

> **1 loaf Sourdough White Bread**
>   **(see Index)**
> **1 pound Danish ham, sliced**
> **1 pound Swiss Cheese,**
>   **shredded**
> **½ cup butter, melted**

Slice bread into 12 slices. Place 3 ounces ham on half of bread slices. Top ham with shredded Swiss cheese. Cover with remaining bread slices.

Melt butter in large skillet. Fry sandwiches on both sides just long enough to brown bread. Serve sandwiches warm.

clam–haddock bake

Yield: 6 to 8 servings

    1 pound haddock fillets
    ½ pound canned clams,
        minced
    ½ cup butter
    ¼ cup chopped onions
    ¼ cup chopped celery
    1 loaf sourdough French Bread
        (see Index), cubed
    2 tablespoons lemon juice
    1 teaspoon salt
    ¼ teaspoon white pepper

Arrange half of haddock fillets close together in a buttered baking dish.
Drain clams, reserving liquid.
Melt butter in skillet. Pour off about half of butter and save it. To butter in skillet add onions and celery and cook them until tender. Stir in bread cubes until butter is soaked up. Continue tossing cubes until they brown slightly. Stir in clams, lemon juice, and enough clam liquid to moisten. Season with salt and pepper.
Spoon stuffing over fillets. Brush them with reserved butter. Bake them in moderate (375° F) oven 20 minutes or until fish flakes easily when tested with fork. Serve it in baking dish.

california dreamers

Yield: 10 to 12 servings

    1 loaf Raisin Whole-Wheat
        Bread (see Index)
    1 8-ounce package cream
        cheese, softened
    1 avocado, peeled and pitted
    4 tablespoons butter, softened
    ¼ cup mayonnaise
    1 teaspoon lemon juice

Slice bread. Combine remaining ingredients in blender. Blend until light and fluffy. Spread filling between bread slices. Portion the sandwiches.

shrimp loaf

A hearty meal for a busy summer afternoon.

Yield: 6 to 8 servings

**1 loaf sourdough French Bread
    (see Index)
2 pounds shrimp, cooked and
    cleaned
Juice of 1 lemon
2 cups chopped celery
2 tablespoons capers
½ cup chopped green pepper
½ cup French dressing
1 cup mayonnaise
1 teaspoon salt
½ teaspoon white pepper**

Slice bread lengthwise. Hollow out centers. (Use centers for fondue.)

Chop shrimps. Combine shrimps, lemon juice, celery, capers, green pepper, French dressing, mayonnaise, salt, and pepper. Toss together.

Fill bottom half of loaf with salad. Cover with top half of loaf. Slice it.

shrimp loaf

beef-filled pancakes

Yield: 12 filled pancakes

**1 recipe Sourdough Oatmeal
   Stacks (see Index)**
1 tablespoon oil
1 clove garlic, crushed
1 onion, chopped
1 pound ground beef
½ teaspoon paprika
1 teaspoon salt
1 tablespoon flour
½ cup milk
1 tablespoon parsley

Make pancakes as directed. Keep them hot on baking sheet in warm oven.

Make filling. Heat oil. Add onion, garlic, meat, paprika, and salt; blend. Add flour; mix well. Add milk gradually. Stir until thickened. Cover pan and simmer mixture 10 minutes, stirring occasionally.

Place 2 tablespoons filling at edge of each pancake and roll them up jelly-roll fashion. Place in chafing dish. Sprinkle with parsley. Serve with a cream sauce.

tuna–mushroom baskets

A quick dinner for your family after a busy day.

Yield: 6 servings

**1 loaf sourdough Honey
   Whole-Wheat Bread (see
   Index)**
½ cup butter, melted
**2 cans cream of mushroom
   soup**
¾ cup milk
2 cans tuna

Trim crusts from large loaf of unsliced bread. Cut bread into blocks 2 × 3 × 2 inches. With sharp knife, cut centers from the blocks, leaving a cavity. Brush the baskets with melted butter. Place on cookie sheet and toast them under broiler until light golden brown.

Combine mushroom soup, milk, and tuna. Heat mixture thoroughly. Pour tuna mixture over bread baskets. Serve immediately.

beef stew with sourdough dumplings

Yield: 6 to 8 servings

 2 pounds beef stew meat, cut
   into 2-inch cubes
 ⅓ cup all-purpose white flour
 5 tablespoons shortening
 1½ teaspoons salt
 ½ teaspoon celery salt
 ¼ teaspoon dry thyme
 1 small clove garlic, finely chopped
 2 cups water
 2 teaspoons Worcestershire sauce
 2 tablespoons catsup
 6 whole cloves
 6 small onions, canned
 1 10-ounce package frozen peas and carrots
 4 potatoes, precooked, cut into 8 wedges each
 ¾ cup all-purpose white flour
 2 teaspoons baking powder
 ¼ teaspoon salt
 ¼ teaspoon baking soda
 ½ cup sourdough starter
 ¼ cup milk

Coat meat on all sides, using ⅓ cup flour. Save extra flour.

Melt 3 tablespoons shortening in heavy kettle. Add meat and brown it well on all sides. Remove browned meat from kettle.

Sprinkle salt, celery salt, thyme, garlic, and extra flour into kettle with shortening, stirring to make a smooth paste. Gradually add water, stirring constantly until gravy is smooth and thickened. Stir in Worcestershire sauce and catsup. Return browned meat to kettle. Cover kettle and cook meat over low heat about 2 hours.

Stick whole cloves into onions. Add onions, peas and carrots, and potatoes to kettle. Cover kettle and continue cooking about 30 minutes or until meat is fork-tender.

Combine flour, baking powder, salt, and baking soda. Cut in remaining 2 tablespoons shortening until mixture resembles cornmeal. Add sourdough starter and milk, stirring enough to blend.

Drop batter by heaping tablespoons on top of stew meat. (Make sure dough is resting on stew meat and not swimming in liquid.) Cover kettle and cook dumplings 10 minutes. Uncover kettle and cook stew another 10 minutes. Serve stew in kettle.

english layered-beef pudding

Yield: 6 servings

> 1 recipe Sourdough White
>   Bread (see Index)
> 1 pound ground beef
> 4 strips bacon, cut into small
>   pieces
> 1 medium onion, chopped
> 1 clove garlic, finely chopped
> 1 teaspoon salt
> ½ teaspoon pepper
> 2 cups grated cheddar cheese
> 2 tomatoes, sliced

Prepare dough; let rise until doubled in bulk. Punch it down. Divide dough into 6 equal parts and roll each section to fit a 2-quart casserole.

Combine ground beef, onion, garlic, and seasonings. Brown the meat mixture. Drain fat.

Arrange meat mixture between layers of dough in an oiled casserole. Sprinkle each layer with ⅓ cup cheese before topping with next layer. Place tomato slices on top layer before adding final ⅓ cup cheese. Bake pudding 30 minutes in 350° F oven or until dough is done and cheese has melted.

beanburgers

Yield: 12 sandwiches

> 2 medium-size onions, sliced
> 2 tablespoons margarine
> 2 cans pork and beans
> 2½ cups spaghetti sauce with
>   meat
> 12 slices processed cheese
> 1 recipe Hamburger Buns (see
>   Index), split and toasted

Brown onions lightly in margarine. Stir in beans and spaghetti sauce; heat thoroughly. Place cheese slices on toasted buns; spoon bean sauce over them. Serve immediately.

carrot timbales

The sourdough bread cubes give added flavor to this vegetable dish.

Yield: 6 servings

2 tablespoons shortening
2 tablespoons all-purpose
white flour
½ teaspoon salt
1½ cups milk
5 large carrots, cut in cubes
3 tablespoons butter
2 cups soft cubes Sourdough
White Bread (see Index)
3 eggs, beaten
1 tablespoon chopped onions
1½ teaspoons salt
1 cup flour
½ cup canned peas
½ teaspoon salt
¼ teaspoon white pepper

Melt shortening in saucepan. Blend in flour and ½ teaspoon salt. Add ½ cup milk and cook mixture until thick, stirring constantly.

Cook carrots in small amount of water until tender. Drain off remaining liquid. Add 2 tablespoons butter to carrots; mash them. Combine mashed carrots with sourdough bread cubes, beaten eggs, onions, and white sauce.

Place mixture into 6 well-greased custard cups. Set custard cups in pan of hot water and bake mixture in 350°F oven 35 minutes.

While timbales are baking, prepare pea sauce. Melt remaining 1 tablespoon butter in small saucepan. Remove it from heat and add flour, stirring with wire whisk. Add remaining 1 cup milk gradually, stirring mixture constantly until sauce has thickened. Stir in peas, salt, and white pepper.

Unmold timbales and serve them with pea sauce.

summer-squash casserole

Yield: 6 servings

6 ounces cheddar cheese, grated
¼ cup butter, melted
3 cups cubed sourdough
Caraway Rye Loaf (see Index)
4 cups summer squash, thinly
sliced
2 tablespoons chopped onions
3 tomatoes, sliced
2 tablespoons chopped green
pepper
½ teaspoon salt
¼ teaspoon white pepper

Grate cheese.

Pour melted butter over rye bread cubes; mix thoroughly.

Grease a 1½-quart casserole. Alternately place layers of squash, onion, tomato, green pepper, cheese, and bread cubes in casserole. Sprinkle with salt and pepper. Repeat process twice, ending with bread cubes.

Cover casserole and bake it in 350° F oven about 1 hour or until vegetables are tender. Serve it hot.

grandma fay's favorite dressing

Yield: 5 to 6 cups

½ pound pork sausage
1 small onion, chopped
½ teaspoon paprika
½ teaspoon salt
½ cup chopped celery
4 cups dried cubes Sourdough
Whole-Wheat Molasses
Bread (see Index)
2 tablespoons parsley
2 tablespoons water

Cook sausage meat and onion, stirring frequently, until onion is lightly browned and sausage is cooked. Combine them with remaining ingredients and mix well.

raisin dressing

An especially fine dressing for chicken, duck, or game birds.

Yield: 4 cups

3 cups dried cubes
    Sourdough White
    Bread (see Index)
1 cup white wine
Liver of bird, chopped
¼ cup chopped onions
2 tablespoons chopped parsley
¼ cup chopped pecans
¼ cup seedless raisins
½ teaspoon sage
¼ teaspoon thyme
½ teaspoon salt
¼ teaspoon pepper
¼ cup butter

Sprinkle bread cubes with wine and squeeze them dry. Reserve excess wine for basting. Combine bread with remaining ingredients in the order given.

chestnut dressing

A traditional Thanksgiving Day dressing.

Yield: About 4 cups

½ pound chestnuts
2 cups dried cubes sourdough
    Honey Whole-Wheat
    Bread (see Index)
¼ cup margarine, melted
1 teaspoon salt
1 teaspoon dried sage
¼ teaspoon pepper
1 egg, beaten
¼ cup half and half

Wash chestnuts and make a gash in each shell. Bake them in very hot oven (500°F) for 15 minutes. Cool them and remove shells and skins. Cook them in boiling salted water for 20 minutes. Drain them and chop them fine. Add remaining ingredients and mix well.

scones and biscuits

bacon scones

Yield: 1 dozen

6 strips bacon
1 cup chopped onions
½ cup sourdough starter
2 cups biscuit mix
⅓ cup milk (approximately)
¼ cup butter, melted

bacon scones

Fry bacon until crisp. Drain and crumble it. Brown onions in bacon fat. Drain them.

Stir sourdough starter into biscuit mix. Add milk until a soft dough forms.

Knead dough 20 times on floured surface. Pat or roll dough to ½ inch thick. Cut it into 12 squares.

Combine crumbled bacon and browned onions. Sprinkle mixture over dough squares. Fold squares in half diagonally. Place on ungreased baking sheet. Brush scones with melted butter.

Bake scones in preheated 450°F oven 10 minutes or until golden brown. Serve them warm.

butter scones

Yield: 1½ dozen

2 cups self-rising flour
½ teaspoon salt
2 tablespoons butter
½ cup cheddar cheese, grated
1 canned pimiento
1 small onion, chopped fine
¼ teaspoon garlic powder
½ cup sourdough starter
¼ cup milk (approximately)
⅓ cup butter, melted

Combine flour and salt. Cut in butter. Add cheese, pimiento, onion, garlic powder, and sourdough starter. Mix with enough milk to make a soft but not sticky dough.

Line bottom of an 8-inch baking dish with waxed paper. Pat out mixture in dish. Bake it at 450°F for 10 minutes or until done. Remove mixture from oven and pour melted butter over it. Let set 5 minutes. Cut it into 1½ × 3-inch fingers. Serve them warm.

sourdough biscuits

Yield: 1 dozen

2 cups all-purpose white flour
2½ teaspoons baking powder
1 teaspoon salt
⅓ cup shortening
½ cup sourdough starter
½ cup milk

Combine dry ingredients. Cut in shortening until mixture resembles dry cornmeal. Add sourdough starter and enough milk to form a soft dough that cleans side of bowl. Knead dough lightly 6 times. Pat or roll it to ½ inch thick. Cut it into biscuits, using a 2½-inch biscuit cutter.

Place biscuits on an ungreased cookie sheet. Bake them in preheated 450° F oven 10 minutes or until golden brown.

jiffy biscuits

Yield: 1 dozen

> ½ **cup sourdough starter**
> **2 cups biscuit mix**
> ⅓ **cup milk (approximately)**

Stir sourdough starter into biscuit mix. Add milk until a soft dough has formed.

Turn out dough onto floured surface and knead 20 times. Pat or roll to ½ inch thick. Cut dough into biscuits, using a 2½-inch biscuit cutter.

Place biscuits on an ungreased cookie sheet and bake them in 450°F oven 10 minutes or until done.

mexican biscuits

Yield: 1 dozen

> **1 cup whole-wheat flour**
> **1 cup all-purpose white flour**
> **2½ teaspoons baking powder**
> **1 teaspoon salt**
> ⅓ **cup shortening**
> ½ **cup sourdough starter**
> ½ **cup milk**
> ½ **cup butter, melted**
> **1 cup Mexican-flavored corn**
>   **chips, crushed fine**

Combine flours, baking powder, and salt. Cut in shortening until mixture resembles dry cornmeal. Add sourdough starter and enough milk to form a soft dough that cleans side of bowl.

Knead dough lightly 6 times. Pat or roll it to ½ inch thick. Cut it into biscuits, using a 2½-inch biscuit cutter. Dip biscuits in melted butter, then in crushed corn chips.

Place biscuits on ungreased cookie sheet. Bake them in preheated 450°F oven 10 minutes or until done.

drop biscuits

Yield: 1 dozen

2 cups all-purpose white flour
2½ teaspoons baking powder
1 teaspoon salt
⅓ cup shortening
½ cup sourdough starter
¾ cup milk

Combine dry ingredients. Cut in shortening until mixture resembles cornmeal. Add sourdough starter and milk. Stir until well-mixed.

Drop batter from a spoon onto greased baking pan and bake biscuits in preheated 450°F oven 10 minutes or until golden brown.

peanut-butter biscuits

Delicious served with ham slices.

Yield: 1½ dozen

2 cups all-purpose white flour
¾ teaspoon salt
2½ teaspoons baking powder
2 tablespoons shortening
¼ cup smooth peanut butter
½ cup sourdough starter
½ cup milk (approximately)

Sift dry ingredients together. Cut in shortening and peanut butter until mixture is like coarse cornmeal. Add sourdough starter and enough milk to form a soft dough.

Roll or pat dough on floured board to ½ inch thick. Cut it with a 2-inch biscuit cutter.

Place biscuits on ungreased baking sheet and bake them in 450°F oven 10 to 12 minutes.

whole-wheat biscuits

Yield: 1 dozen

1 cup whole-wheat flour
1 cup all-purpose white flour
2½ teaspoons baking powder
1 teaspoon salt
⅓ cup shortening
½ cup sourdough starter
½ cup milk

Combine dry ingredients. Cut in shortening until mixture resembles dry cornmeal. Add sourdough starter and enough milk to form a soft dough that cleans side of bowl. Knead dough lightly 6 times. Pat or roll it to ½ inch thick. Cut it into biscuits, using a 2½-inch biscuit cutter.

Place biscuits on an ungreased cookie sheet. Bake them in preheated 450°F oven 10 minutes or until golden brown.

biscuit crackers

This Southern treat has a texture all its own.

Yield: 1 dozen

1¾ cups self-rising flour
1 tablespoon granulated sugar
¼ cup shortening
½ cup sourdough starter
½ cup water

Blend flour and sugar. Cut in shortening until mixture resembles cornmeal. Add sourdough starter and enough water to make a stiff dough.

Turn out dough onto floured surface. Knead it 20 minutes, then pound it with your fists 5 more minutes. Pat dough to ½ inch thick. Cut it into rounds. Prick tops with a fork.

Bake crackers at 400°F for 20 minutes or until lightly brown. They are best if served warm.

italian biscuit sticks

Yield: 10 sticks

> 1 5½-ounce package
>   buttermilk biscuit mix
> ⅓ cup Sourdough Starter II
>   (see Index)
> 2 to 3 tablespoons water
> ½ cup margarine, melted
> ¼ teaspoon garlic powder
> ¼ cup sesame seeds

Combine biscuit mix, sourdough starter, and water. Stir to blend.

With floured hands knead about 5 times on floured surface. Divide dough into 10 equal balls. With floured hands roll balls into oblong sticks.

Combine melted margarine and garlic powder. Roll sticks in garlic–margarine mixture and then in sesame seeds.

Place sticks on lightly greased baking sheet. Bake them 10 to 12 minutes in 450°F oven. Serve them warm.

raisin mounds

Yield: 1 dozen

> 1 cup whole-wheat flour
> 1 cup all-purpose white flour
> 2½ teaspoons baking powder
> 1 teaspoon salt
> ⅓ cup shortening
> ½ cup sourdough starter
> ¾ cup milk
> ½ cup raisins

Combine dry ingredients. Cut in shortening until mixture resembles cornmeal. Add sourdough starter and milk. Stir in raisins.

Drop batter from a spoon onto greased baking pan and bake mounds in preheated 450°F oven 10 minutes or until golden brown.

swiss-cheese squares

swiss-cheese squares

Yield: 1½ dozen

2 cups all-purpose white flour
2½ teaspoons baking powder
½ teaspoon baking soda
1 teaspoon salt
⅓ cup shortening

½ cup sourdough starter
½ cup buttermilk
1 cup grated Swiss cheese
1 egg, beaten
3 tablespoons poppy seeds

Combine flour, baking powder, baking soda, and salt. Cut in shortening until mixture resembles dry cornmeal. Add sourdough starter and enough milk to form a soft dough that cleans side of bowl. Add Swiss cheese. Knead Swiss cheese lightly into dough. Pat or roll dough to ½ inch thick. Cut into squares, using a scalloped knife or a cookie cutter. Brush tops with beaten egg. Sprinkle with poppy seeds.

Place squares on ungreased cookie sheet. Bake them in preheated 450°F oven 10 minutes or until golden brown.

poppy–nut cake

An American version of German Mohn cake.

Yield: 1 cake

¼ cup brandy
1 cup raisins
2 12-ounce cans poppy-seed filling
1 cup almonds, chopped
2 cups all-purpose white flour
2½ teaspoons baking powder
1 teaspoon salt
⅓ cup shortening
½ cup sourdough starter
½ cup milk
½ cup butter, melted

Combine brandy and raisins. Let raisins soak until brandy is absorbed by them. Stir poppy-seed filling and nuts into raisins. Set mixture aside.

Combine dry ingredients. Cut in shortening until mixture resembles dry cornmeal. Add sourdough starter and enough milk to form a soft dough that cleans side of bowl.

Knead dough lightly 6 times. Pat or roll it to ½ inch thick. Cut it into biscuits, using a 2½-inch biscuit cutter.

Grease baking dish. Layer biscuits, topping each layer with melted butter and poppy-seed mixture, ending with poppy-seed mixture.

Bake cake in 375°F oven 20 minutes or until done.

poppy–nut cake

cherry ring

Yield: 8 servings

2 cups all-purpose white flour
2½ teaspoons baking powder
1 teaspoon salt
⅓ cup shortening
½ cup sourdough starter
½ cup milk
¼ cup butter, melted
¼ cup granulated sugar
1 teaspoon cinnamon
¼ cup chopped nuts
¾ cup cherry preserves

Combine flour, baking powder, and salt. Cut in shortening until mixture resembles cornmeal. Add sourdough starter and enough milk to form a soft dough that cleans side of bowl.

Knead lightly 6 times. Roll dough into a ¼-inch-thick rectangle. Spread with melted butter, and sprinkle with sugar, cinnamon, and nuts. Roll dough jelly-roll fashion; shape it into a ring on greased cookie sheet. Press ends together. Using scissors, snip from outer edge almost to center at 1-inch intervals. Turn each cut slice on its side so that cut surface is up. Place 1 teaspoon cherry preserves in center of each slice.

Bake ring in preheated 450°F oven 15 minutes or until golden brown.

fried dough

quick doughnuts

quick doughnuts

Yield: 2 dozen

> **4½ teaspoons baking powder**
> **2 teaspoons salt**
> **1 tablespoon granulated sugar**
> **4 cups all-purpose white flour**
> **⅔ cup shortening**
> **1 cup sourdough starter**
> **1 cup milk**
> **1 cup granulated sugar**

Combine first 4 ingredients. Cut in shortening until mixture resembles dry cornmeal. Add sourdough starter and enough milk to form a soft dough that cleans side of bowl.

Knead dough lightly 6 times. Pat or roll dough to ½ inch thick. Cut it into biscuits, using a 2½-inch biscuit cutter.

Fry doughnuts in grease preheated to 360°F for 1½ minutes or until golden brown. Drain them. Sprinkle with granulated sugar.

granola doughnuts

granola doughnuts

Yield: 2 dozen

1½ cups flour
¼ cup granulated sugar
1 teaspoon salt
½ teaspoon baking soda
1 teaspoon baking powder
1 teaspoon nutmeg

½ cup sourdough starter
1 egg, beaten
½ cup milk
¼ cup oil
½ cup Granola with Raisins
Oil for frying

Combine first 6 ingredients. Add sourdough starter, egg, milk, and ¼ cup oil to dry ingredients. Beat until smooth. Add Granola; mix well.

Heat frying oil to 360°F. Drop batter by teaspoonfuls into hot fat. Fry doughnuts 1½ minutes or until done. Drain them on paper grocery bag. Roll them in cinnamon–sugar mixture.

sugar and cinnamon coating

Yield: Coating for 3- to 4-dozen doughnuts

2 cups granulated sugar
2 teaspoons cinnamon

Combine sugar and cinnamon in medium-size paper bag. Shake to mix. Place drained doughnuts in paper bag. Shake to coat doughnuts on all sides. Remove doughnuts from bag and place on cooling rack.

polish doughnuts

Yield: 5 dozen

2 cups milk
1 package active dry yeast
½ cup sourdough starter
3 eggs, whipped until light
    and fluffy
½ cup oil
1 tablespoon vanilla
½ cup granulated sugar
1 teaspoon salt
2 cups all-purpose white flour
5 to 5½ cups all-purpose flour
Oil for frying

Scald milk. Cool it to lukewarm. Dissolve yeast in milk. Mix in sourdough starter. Let set 12 hours or overnight to develop sponge.

Add eggs, oil, vanilla, sugar, and salt. Mix well. Stir in 2 cups flour.

Pour 1 cup flour on kneading surface. Pour sponge on top of flour; cover sponge with 1 cup flour. Knead in flour. Continue adding flour until a medium-stiff dough has formed. Knead for 10 minutes or until dough becomes elastic.

Place dough in greased bowl. Grease top. Cover dough. Let rise until doubled in bulk.

Punch down dough. Knead for 2 minutes. Roll dough to ½ inch thick and cut doughnuts. Place doughnuts on greased cookie sheet and let rise until doubled in bulk.

Heat frying oil to 360°F. Fry doughnuts until golden brown (about 1½ minutes on each side). Drain excess fat from doughnuts on brown-paper grocery bag. Glaze with Cream Glaze.

cream glaze

Yield: Glaze for 5- to 6-dozen doughnuts

> 1 pound powdered sugar
> 1 tablespoon cornstarch
> 1 tablespoon cream
> 1 teaspoon vanilla
> 2 tablespoons water
>   (approximately)

Combine sugar, cornstarch, cream, and vanilla. Add water to make a mixture of medium consistency. Dip warm doughnuts in glaze.

banana doughnuts

Yield: 3½ dozen

> 5 cups all-purpose white flour
> 4 teaspoons baking powder
> 1 teaspoon soda
> 2 teaspoons salt
> 1 teaspoon cinnamon
> ¼ cup margarine
> 1 cup granulated sugar
> 3 eggs, well-beaten
> ¾ cup mashed bananas
> ⅓ cup milk
> ½ cup sourdough starter
> Oil for deep-fat frying

Sift together flour, baking powder, baking soda, salt, and cinnamon.

Beat margarine until creamy. Add sugar gradually and continue beating until light and fluffy. Add eggs and beat well.

Combine bananas, milk, and sourdough starter; add to creamed mixture. Add flour mixture and mix until smooth.

Turn a small amount of dough onto lightly floured board. Knead very lightly. Roll dough to ½ inch thick. Cut it with a floured 2½-inch doughnut cutter. Deep-fat fry doughnuts at 375°F for 3 minutes or until golden brown. Drain them on brown-paper grocery bag. Glaze if desired.

sourdough raised doughnuts

sourdough raised doughnuts

Yield: 3 dozen

1 package active dry yeast
½ cup warm water
1 cup sourdough starter
½ cup milk
⅓ cup margarine
1 cup granulated sugar

1 teaspoon salt
2 eggs, beaten
1 cup mashed potatoes
4½ to 5 cups all-purpose white
    flour

Dissolve yeast in water. Stir in sourdough starter.

Scald milk; add margarine, sugar, and salt. Let mixture cool. Add beaten eggs, sourdough mixture, and mashed potatoes. Mix until potatoes are blended into mixture. Stir in flour to make a medium-soft dough. Cover dough. Let rise until doubled in bulk.

Punch down dough and knead on floured surface 5 minutes. Place in greased bowl, cover, and let rise again until doubled in bulk.

Place dough on well-floured surface. Roll to ½ inch thick, cut with a 2-inch doughnut cutter, and let rise again until doubled in size.

Heat 1 quart oil to 360°F. Fry doughnuts until golden brown (about 1½ minutes on each side). On brown-paper grocery bag drain excess fat from doughnuts. Glaze or sugar them if desired.

lichter's drop doughnuts

Yield: 2 dozen

1¾ cups all-purpose white flour
¼ cup granulated sugar
1 teaspoon salt
¼ cup margarine, melted
1 egg, beaten
½ teaspoon soda

1 teaspoon baking powder
½ cup milk
½ cup sourdough starter
Oil for frying
1 teaspoon nutmeg
1 cup granulated sugar

Mix ingredients as listed, excluding nutmeg and 1 cup sugar.

Heat frying oil to 350°F. Drop doughnuts by teaspoonfuls into hot oil. Fry them about 90 seconds or until done. Drain them on brown-paper grocery bag.

Combine nutmeg and 1 cup of sugar. Roll drained doughnuts in sugar and cinnamon. Cool them on a rack.

apricot fried cakes

Yield: 3½ dozen

½ cup cream
1 package active dry yeast
½ cup sourdough starter
1 tablespoon sugar
3 egg yolks, beaten
1 tablespoon brandy

½ teaspoon salt
3 to 4 cups all-purpose white flour
3 cups apricot preserves
Oil for frying

Scald cream. Cool it to lukewarm. Dissolve yeast in cream. Add sourdough starter. Let set 1 hour.

Add sugar, egg yolks, brandy, and salt; mix well. Work in enough flour to develop a soft dough.

Knead for 10 minutes or until dough becomes elastic. Place in greased bowl. Grease top of dough. Cover it. Let rise until doubled in bulk.

Punch down dough. Roll it to ½ inch thick. Cut it into 3-inch squares. Place a spoonful of apricot preserves on one half of each square. Lap other half of square over filling. Seal edges. Let rise 30 minutes in warm place.

Heat oil to 360°F. Fry cakes until golden brown. Drain excess grease.

fried braids

fried braids

Yield: 4 dozen

2 cups milk
1 package active dry yeast
½ cup sourdough starter
2 eggs, whipped until fluffy
½ cup shortening, melted
½ cup honey

1 teaspoon salt
2 cups all-purpose white flour
5 to 5½ cups all-purpose white flour
Oil for frying
1 cup powdered sugar, sifted

Scald milk. Cool it to lukewarm. Dissolve yeast in milk. Add sourdough starter. Mix well. Let set 12 hours or overnight to develop sponge.

Add eggs, shortening, honey, and salt. Mix well. Stir in 2 cups flour.

Pour 1 cup flour on kneading surface. Pour sponge on top of flour; cover sponge with 1 cup flour. Knead in flour. Continue adding flour until a medium-stiff dough has formed. Knead for 10 minutes or until dough becomes elastic. Place in greased bowl. Grease top. Cover dough. Let rise until doubled in bulk.

Punch down dough. Knead for 2 minutes. Roll dough to ½ inch thick and cut it into 1 × 4-inch strips. Roll each strip to form a rod shape. Form braids. Place braids on greased cookie sheet. Cover them. Let rise until doubled in bulk.

Heat frying oil to 360°F. Fry braids until golden brown. Drain them. Dust them with powdered sugar.

111

jelly bismarcks

jelly bismarcks

Yield: 1 dozen

2 cups all-purpose white flour
2½ teaspoons baking powder
2 teaspoons granulated sugar
1 teaspoon salt
½ teaspoon cinnamon
⅓ cup shortening
½ cup sourdough starter
½ cup milk
¾ cup apricot preserves
1 tablespoon rum
1 cup granulated sugar
Oil for deep-fat frying

Combine dry ingredients, except 1 cup sugar. Cut in shortening until mixture resembles dry cornmeal. Add sourdough starter and enough milk to form a soft dough that cleans side of bowl.

Knead dough lightly 6 times. Pat or roll it to ¼ inch thick. Cut it into biscuit rounds.

Combine apricot preserves and rum. Place 1 tablespoon apricot–rum mixture in middle of half of rounds. Top with remaining rounds. Crimp edges.

Deep-fat fry rounds at 360°F about 2 minutes or until golden brown. Drain them. Sprinkle with granulated sugar while they are still warm.

jeff's chocolate nuggets

Yield: 2½ dozen

jeff's chocolate nuggets

    1¾ cups flour
    ¼ cup cocoa
    ½ cup granulated sugar
    1 teaspoon salt
    1 teaspoon cinnamon
    ¼ cup butter, melted
    1 egg, beaten
    ½ teaspoon soda
    1 teaspoon baking powder
    ½ cup milk
    ½ cup sourdough starter
    1 cup raisins
    Oil for frying

Mix ingredients as listed.

Heat frying oil to 360°F. Drop batter by small teaspoonfuls into hot oil. Fry them about 1½ minutes or until done. Turn them once during frying. Drain them on brown-paper grocery sack. Dip tops of warm nuggets into Sour-Cream Chocolate Glaze. Cool them on a rack.

sour-cream chocolate glaze

Yield: Glaze for 2½- to 3-dozen doughnuts

    4 cups powdered sugar (1 box)
    2 tablespoons cornstarch
    2 ounces unsweetened baking
        chocolate, melted
    ¼ cup sour cream
    3 to 4 tablespoons milk

Combine powdered sugar and cornstarch in medium-size mixing bowl. Add chocolate, sour cream, and milk. Blend until smooth.

kansas long johns

Yield: 3 dozen

¾ cup milk
1 package active dry yeast
1 cup sourdough starter
⅓ cup butter, melted
1 cup granulated sugar
1 teaspoon salt
2 eggs, beaten until fluffy
1 cup mashed potatoes
4½ to 5 cups all-purpose white
    flour
2 packages vanilla pudding
    mix
1 quart milk
Oil for frying

Scald ¾ cup milk. Cool it to lukewarm. Dissolve yeast in milk. Stir in sourdough starter. Add butter, sugar, salt, and eggs. Stir in mashed potatoes. Mix well, until all potatoes are dissolved. Stir in flour to make a medium-soft dough. Cover dough. Let rise until doubled in bulk.

Punch down dough. Knead for an additional 5 minutes. Cover dough. Let it rise again until doubled in bulk.

Place dough on well-floured surface and roll it to ½ inch thick. Cut it into 2 × 4-inch strips. Place on greased cookie sheet. Cover them. Let rise until doubled in bulk.

While Long Johns are rising, prepare pudding.

Heat frying oil to 360°F. Fry Long Johns until golden brown. Drain excess fat on brown-paper grocery bag. Split Long Johns in half lengthwise. Fill with 2 tablespoons vanilla pudding. Glaze with Sour-Cream Chocolate Glaze.

Picture on opposite page: kansas long johns

blueberry fritters

Yield: 6 servings

1 cup all-purpose white flour	2 tablespoons milk
1 teaspoon baking powder	1 tablespoon oil
½ teaspoon salt	1½ cups fresh blueberries
1 tablespoon granulated sugar	2 egg whites, stiffly beaten
2 egg yolks	Oil for frying
½ cup sourdough starter	

Sift together flour, baking powder, salt, and sugar.

Combine egg yolks, sourdough starter, milk, and 1 tablespoon oil. Add mixture to dry ingredients; mix until well-blended. Add fruit. Fold in stiffly beaten egg whites.

Heat frying oil to 375°F. Drop fritters by tablespoonfuls into hot oil and fry them 3 to 4 minutes, turning them to brown evenly. Drain excess grease. Serve them with warm syrup.

corn fritters

Yield: 6 servings

½ cup all-purpose white flour	2 tablespoons milk
½ cup whole-wheat flour	1 tablespoon margarine, melted
1 teaspoon baking powder	
½ teaspoon salt	2 cups whole-kernel corn
1 tablespoon granulated sugar	2 egg whites, stiffly beaten
2 egg yolks	Oil for frying
½ cup sourdough starter	

Sift together flours, baking powder, salt, and sugar.

Combine egg yolks, sourdough starter, milk, and margarine. Add mixture to dry ingredients; mix until well-blended. Add corn. Fold in stiffly beaten egg whites.

Heat oil to 375°F. Drop fritters by tablespoonfuls into hot oil and fry them 3 to 4 minutes, turning them to brown evenly. Drain excess grease. Serve them warm.

desserts

easter bunny cake

Yield: 2 8-inch layers

- ½ cup sourdough starter
- 1 cup warm water
- 1½ cups all-purpose white flour
- ¼ cup powdered nonfat dry milk
- 1 cup brown sugar, packed firmly
- ½ cup margarine
- ½ teaspoon salt
- 1 teaspoon cinnamon
- 1½ teaspoons baking soda
- ½ cup plus 2 tablespoons cocoa
- 1 teaspoon vanilla
- 2 eggs, beaten
- ½ cup raisins
- 1 cup pecans, chopped
- 2 cups powdered-sugar white icing
- 1 rabbit cookie cutter

easter bunny cake

Combine sourdough starter, warm water, 1¼ cups flour, and dry milk. Let stand inside an unheated oven 2 hours.

Cream together brown sugar and margarine. Gradually add salt, cinnamon, baking soda, cocoa, and vanilla to creamed mixture. Blend until smooth. Add creamed mixture and eggs to starter mixture. Mix in electric mixer at low speed 2 minutes or until blended.

Combine raisins, nuts, and remaining ¼ cup flour. Toss until raisins and nuts are coated with flour. Stir them into cake batter.

Pour batter into 2 8-inch greased cake pans. Bake cake at 350°F for 25 to 30 minutes. Remove it from cake pans and cool it on racks.

Place bottom layer of cake on serving dish. Frost top with ¼ cup frosting. Place top layer on top of first layer. Center rabbit cookie cutter in center of cake. Frost outside of cake with remaining icing. Remove cookie cutter and form rabbit's eye with a dot of frosting.

mama boor's caramel bread sponge cake with apricot sauce

Yield: One 8 × 12-inch sheet cake

½ cup sourdough starter
1 cup warm water
1¾ cups plus 2 tablespoons
    all-purpose white flour
¼ cup powdered nonfat dry
    milk
1 cup brown sugar, packed
½ cup butter
½ teaspoon salt

1½ teaspoons baking soda
1 teaspoon cinnamon
1 teaspoon nutmeg
1 teaspoon allspice
1 teaspoon vanilla
1 cup raisins
1 cup chopped English
    walnuts

Combine sourdough starter, water, 1½ cups flour, and milk. Set mixture in unheated oven for 2 hours.

Cream together brown sugar and butter. Gradually add salt, baking soda, spices, and vanilla to creamed mixture. Blend until smooth. Add creamed mixture to starter mixture. Mix in electric mixer at low speed 2 minutes or until blended.

Combine raisins, nuts, and remaining flour. Toss until raisins and nuts are coated with flour. Stir them into cake batter.

Pour batter into greased 8 × 12-inch pan. Bake cake at 350°F for 50 minutes or until done. Serve with Apricot Sauce.

apricot sauce

Yield: 2 cups

2 10-ounce jars apricot
    preserves
Juice and rind of 2 lemons
¼ teaspoon cinnamon

Pinch of cloves
2 teaspoons arrowroot
2 tablespoons cold water

Melt apricot preserves in small heavy saucepan, adding lemon juice, rind, and spices. Strain contents of pan and put the clear liquid into clean saucepan.

Dissolve arrowroot in cold water and add it to sauce. As sauce comes to boiling point, it will thicken. Serve it over Mama Boor's Caramel Bread Sponge Cake.

Picture on opposite page: apple cake

apple cake

Yield: 1 10-inch-round cake

2 tablespoons margarine	¾ cup milk
1 cup granulated sugar	½ cup sourdough starter
1 egg, beaten	2 large apples, peeled and
2 cups all-purpose white flour	sliced thin
2 teaspoons baking powder	2 tablespoons margarine,
1 teaspoon salt	melted
¼ teaspoon nutmeg	2 tablespoons granulated sugar
½ teaspoon cinnamon	½ cup whipping cream

Cream margarine and 1 cup granulated sugar; add egg and beat well.

Combine flour, baking powder, salt, and spices.

Combine milk and sourdough starter.

Add dry mixture and liquids alternately to creamed mixture. Pour batter into greased 10-inch-round, 2-inch-deep cake pan. Arrange apples in a ring design as illustrated.

Pour melted margarine over apples, sprinkle with 2 tablespoons sugar, and place in moderate (375°F) oven. Bake cake for ½ hour, then pour cream over cake and return it to oven to continue baking for another ½ hour or until cake tests done with a toothpick.

14-karat cake

Yield: One 9 × 12-inch sheet cake

1 cup whole-wheat flour	2 teaspoons baking soda
1 cup all-purpose white flour	½ cup sourdough starter
2 teaspoons cinnamon	1 cup cooking oil
1 teaspoon salt	4 eggs, beaten
2 cups granulated sugar	3 cups grated carrots

Mix dry ingredients.

Pour oil into large mixing bowl. Add sourdough starter. Add dry ingredients and eggs. Mix until smooth. Stir in grated carrots.

Pour batter in greased and floured 9 × 12-inch cake pan. Bake it in preheated 350°F oven 40 to 45 minutes or until done. Cool cake. Frost with cream-cheese frosting.

black-walnut cake

A light dessert to serve at the end of a hearty meal.

Yield: One 8 × 12-inch cake

1 cup margarine	4 teaspoons baking powder
1¼ cups granulated sugar	½ teaspoon salt
½ cup brown sugar, packed	1 cup sourdough starter
2 eggs	½ cup milk
2⅓ cups all-purpose white flour	1 teaspoon cinnamon
	1 cup chopped black walnuts

Cream margarine, 1 cup granulated sugar, and brown sugar until light and fluffy. Beat in eggs, 1 at a time.

Combine flour, baking powder, and salt.

Combine starter and milk.

Add dry mixture and starter mixture alternately to creamed mixture until all ingredients are blended well.

Lightly grease and flour an 8 × 12-inch cake pan. Pour batter into greased pan.

Combine remaining ¼ cup sugar, cinnamon, and black walnuts. Sprinkle over batter.

Place cake in middle of 350°F oven and bake it 50 minutes or until a toothpick inserted in center comes out clean. To serve, cut it into 2-inch squares.

honey cake with peach sauce

Yield: 12 servings

    2½ cups all-purpose white
        flour
    1 teaspoon salt
    1 teaspoon baking soda
    3 tablespoons butter
    1 cup honey
    1 egg, beaten
    ½ cup sourdough starter
    ⅔ cup milk
    1 pint whipping cream,
        whipped

Sift dry ingredients together.

Cream butter and honey.

Combine milk and sourdough starter.

Add dry ingredients alternately with sourdough-starter mixture and eggs to honey mixture.

Pour batter into greased 9-inch loaf pan. Bake cake at 300°F for 1 hour and 40 minutes. Cool it. Cut cake into 12 equal slices. Top each slice with ⅓ cup Peach Sauce. Garnish with whipped cream.

peach sauce

Yield: Approximately 4 cups

    1 cup granulated sugar
    2 cups water
    Juice of ½ lemon
    12 strips lemon rind
    6 ripe peaches or ½ pound
        dried peaches soaked
        overnight in water

Make a syrup by combining sugar and water. Add lemon juice and rind. Simmer peaches in syrup 10 minutes. Remove peaches and press them through a sieve or puree them in a blender, adding a little of the syrup in which peaches were poached to correct consistency of sauce.

almond cakes

almond cakes

Yield: Three 9-inch layers

1 cup butter	**½ teaspoon salt**
½ cup granulated sugar	**1 cup sourdough starter**
1 cup brown sugar, packed	**½ cup milk**
4 egg yolks, beaten	**¾ cup granulated sugar**
2⅓ cups all-purpose white flour	**2 teaspoons cinnamon**
4 teaspoons baking powder	**2 cups slivered almonds**

Cream butter, ½ cup granulated sugar, and brown sugar until light and fluffy. Beat in egg yolks.

Combine flour, baking powder, and salt.

Combine starter and milk.

Add dry mixture and starter mixture alternately to creamed mixture until all ingredients are blended well.

Lightly grease and flour 3 9-inch cake pans. Pour batter into greased pans.

Combine ¾ cup sugar, cinnamon, and almonds. Sprinkle over batter.

Place cakes in preheated 350°F oven; bake them 30 to 40 minutes or until a toothpick inserted in center comes out clean.

russian christmas cake

Yield: 3 loaves

2 teaspoons baking soda
1 8-ounce package dates, cut up
2 cups boiling water
1 cup margarine
1 cup brown sugar, packed
1 cup granulated sugar

2 eggs, beaten
½ cup sourdough starter
2¾ cups all-purpose white
    flour
⅓ cup wheat germ
2 cups chopped pecans

Mix baking soda and dates. Pour boiling water over dates and let stand until cool.

Cream margarine and sugars. Add eggs and beat until smooth.

Combine sourdough starter and date mixture.

Combine flour and wheat germ. Alternately add dates and flour mixture to creamed mixture, mixing well after each addition. Fold in pecans.

Pour batter into 3 well-greased and floured loaf pans. Bake loaves at 375°F for 10 minutes, then lower temperature to 350°F and bake them 50 minutes more or until done. Remove loaves from oven. Let stand 10 minutes before removing them from pans.

cherry-chocolate cake

Yield: Two 8-inch layers

½ cup sourdough starter
1 cup warm water
1½ cups all-purpose white
    flour
½ cup powdered nonfat dry
    milk
1 cup brown sugar, packed
½ cup margarine

½ teaspoon salt
1½ teaspoons baking soda
½ cup plus 2 tablespoons
    cocoa
1 teaspoon vanilla
2 eggs, beaten
1 can cherry-pie filling
1 pint cream, whipped

Combine starter, warm water, flour, and dry milk. Set mixture inside unheated oven for 2 hours or until it becomes bubbly on top.

Cream together brown sugar and margarine. Gradually add salt, baking soda, cocoa, and vanilla to creamed mixture. Blend until smooth. Add creamed mixture and eggs to starter mixture. Mix in electric mixer at low speed 2 minutes or until blended.

Pour batter into 2 8-inch greased and floured layer-cake pans. Bake cake at 350°F for 25 to 30 minutes. Remove it from cake pans and cool it on rack. Place 1 layer of cake on serving plate. Spread it with ½ can cherry-pie filling. Top with remaining layer of cake. Spread remaining pie filling on top of cake. Slice it and serve with whipped cream.

potica

Yield: 12 to 16 servings

1 package active dry yeast
1 cup warm water
1 cup sourdough starter
1 cup all-purpose white flour
¼ cup butter, melted
1¼ cups granulated sugar
1 teaspoon salt
1 egg, beaten
3¼ to 3½ cups all-purpose
    white flour
2 cups walnuts, chopped
1 teaspoon cinnamon
3 tablespoons granulated sugar
½ cup chopped dates
¾ cup milk
3 egg whites, beaten stiff
1 cup powdered sugar

potica

Dissolve yeast in warm water. Add sourdough starter. Blend thoroughly. Mix in 1 cup flour. Cover mixture. Set it in warm place 12 hours or overnight.

Stir sponge to dissolve crust. Add butter, ¼ cup sugar, and salt. Mix well. Blend in egg. Add flour until a soft dough has formed. Pour remaining flour on kneading surface. Work remaining flour into dough. Knead about 10 minutes or until folds form in dough. Place dough ball in greased bowl. Grease top of dough ball. Cover it. Let rise until doubled in bulk.

While dough is rising, blend walnuts, cinnamon, 3 tablespoons sugar, dates, and milk in saucepan. Cook them over medium heat, stirring until mixture thickens. Remove it from heat and cool it.

Beat egg whites until stiff and slowly add 1 cup granulated sugar, beating until meringue-like. Fold this into walnut mixture.

Punch down dough. Knead for 2 minutes. Divide dough into 2 equal parts. Roll out each dough piece to make a circle 20 inches in diameter. Top rolled dough with half of filling mixture, spreading it to within 1 inch of edges. Carefully roll up dough, jelly-roll fashion. Place roll in well-greased tube pan. Roll out and fill second portion of dough in same manner and place on top of first roll. Allow to rise for 45 minutes.

Bake potica at 350°F about 1 hour or until a toothpick inserted in center comes out clean. Let cool 5 minutes before turning it out. Dust top of warm cake with powdered sugar.

124

lebkuchen

lebkuchen

Yield: 2-dozen cookies

1 cup chopped walnuts
½ cup mixed glacé fruit
¼ teaspoon orange peel
1¾ cups all-purpose white
 flour
½ teaspoon baking soda
½ teaspoon salt
½ teaspoon allspice

½ teaspoon nutmeg
1 teaspoon cinnamon
1 teaspoon freeze-dried coffee
½ cup margarine
¼ cup brown sugar, packed
1 egg, beaten
⅓ cup honey
½ cup sourdough starter

Mix walnuts, fruit, and orange peel.

Combine flour, baking soda, spices, and coffee; sprinkle over fruit-and-nut mixture.

Cream margarine and brown sugar until fluffy; beat in egg. Add honey and sourdough starter alternately with flour-and-nut mixture. Mix well.

Spread batter on greased jelly-roll pan and bake it in preheated 375°F oven 15 minutes or until done. Remove cookies from oven and frost with Rum Glaze. Cool them. Cut them into bars.

rum glaze

Yield: Approximately 1 cup

¼ cup water
1 cup powdered sugar
1 teaspoon rum flavoring

Combine all ingredients and mix well.

camping cookies

A quick and easy dessert for a camping trip.

Yield: 45 cookies

1 loaf Banana Wheat Bread   **1 12-ounce package chocolate**
    (see Index)   **chips**
                                       1 cup coconut

Remove crust from all 4 sides of loaf of bread. Cut remaining loaf into 3 × 6 × 2-inch strips.

Melt chocolate chips in shallow skillet. Cool them to lukewarm. Using tongs, coat bread strips with warm chocolate, making sure all sides are covered. Remove strips from chocolate, and roll them in coconut. Place on waxed paper to set the chocolate.

south american cakes

Yield: 4-dozen cookies

½ cup butter   **¾ teaspoon baking powder**
1 cup brown sugar   **½ teaspoon salt**
1 egg, beaten   **1 teaspoon allspice**
1 teaspoon vanilla   **⅓ cup milk**
1 cup all-purpose white flour   **½ cup sourdough starter**
1 cup whole-wheat flour   **1 cup Brazil nuts, chopped**
¾ teaspoon baking soda

Cream butter and brown sugar; mix in egg and vanilla.

Combine dry ingredients.

Combine milk and sourdough starter; add alternately with dry ingredients to creamed mixture. Add nuts.

Drop batter by teaspoonfuls onto greased cookie sheet, 2 inches apart. Bake them at 400°F for 8 to 10 minutes. Cool them.

blueberry cobbler

Yield: 6 servings

1 cup all-purpose flour
2 tablespoons brown sugar
1½ teaspoons baking powder
½ teaspoon salt
2 tablespoons margarine,
    chilled and crumbled

⅔ cup sourdough starter
1 can blueberry-pie filling
1 tablespoon margarine,
    melted

Combine flour, brown sugar, baking powder, and salt in large mixing bowl. Add chilled margarine, and, with your fingertips, work mixture until it resembles a coarse meal. Pour in sourdough starter until a soft dough forms.

Gather dough into a ball and knead it for 2 minutes. On floured surface roll dough into an 8 × 8-inch square. Cut it into 6 rectangles measuring approximately 2½ × 4 inches.

Spread blueberry-pie filling in greased dish. Arrange dough rectangles over pie filling. Brush dough with melted margarine. Bake it in preheated 425°F oven 25 to 30 minutes or until dough is golden brown. Serve it warm with whipped cream.

butterscotch fingers

An unusual blend of butterscotch and bananas.

Yield: 45 cookies

1 loaf Banana Wheat Bread
    (see Index)
2 6-ounce packages
    butterscotch chips
1 cup walnuts, chopped

Remove crust from all 4 sides of loaf of bread. Cut remaining loaf into 3 × 6 × 2-inch strips.

Melt butterscotch chips in shallow pan. Cool them to lukewarm. Using tongs, coat bread strips with warm butterscotch, making sure all sides are covered. Remove strips from butterscotch sauce, and roll them in nuts. Place on waxed paper to set the sauce.

As a variation, the bread may be cubed and dipped in sauce as in fondue and then coated with nuts.

apple brown betty

Delicious served with Lemon Sauce.

Yield: 6 servings

½ cup raisins
½ cup water
4 cooking apples, peeled,
    cored, and thinly sliced
3 cups sourdough French
    Bread (see Index) crumbs
¾ cup granulated sugar
⅛ teaspoon nutmeg
1 teaspoon cinnamon
½ cup margarine

Combine raisins and water. Cook them until water is absorbed by raisins. Combine sugar, nutmeg, cinnamon, and raisins.

Arrange apples and bread crumbs in layers in 8 × 8-inch greased pan. Sprinkle raisin mixture over each layer. Pour margarine over top layer of apples and crumbs.

Bake mixture at 350°F for 30 minutes or until apples are cooked. Serve it hot with Lemon Sauce.

lemon sauce

Yield: 6 servings

1 tablespoon butter
1 cup boiling water
½ cup granulated sugar
2 whole eggs
Juice of 1 lemon
1 tablespoon cornstarch
1 teaspoon vanilla

Melt butter in water with half of sugar.

In separate bowl combine eggs and remaining sugar with lemon juice. Add cornstarch. Pour boiling water, sugar, and melted butter into egg mixture and stir over gentle heat until thickened. Add vanilla. Serve sauce over warm Apple Brown Betty.

caviar rounds

caviar rounds

Yield: 20 rounds

> 2 cups sifted flour
> ¾ teaspoon salt
> 2½ teaspoons baking powder
> ⅓ cup shortening
> ½ cup sourdough starter
> ½ cup milk (approximately)
> 1 cup caviar

Sift dry ingredients together. Cut in shortening until mixture is like coarse cornmeal. Add sourdough starter and enough milk to form a soft dough.

Roll or pat dough on floured board to ½ inch thick. Cut it with 1¼-inch-round biscuit cutter. Place half of the biscuits on an ungreased cookie sheet. With ¾-inch biscuit cutter, cut centers from remaining circles. Place rings on top of biscuits.

Bake rounds in 450°F oven 10 to 12 minutes or until golden brown. Remove them from oven and fill center wells with caviar.

french bread fondue

Yield: 16 servings

1 cup white wine (Chablis or California white wine)
2 whole cloves garlic, peeled
¾ pound Swiss cheese, grated
3 tablespoons flour
Freshly ground black pepper

3 tablespoons kirsch
3 tablespoons butter
¼ cup heavy cream
1 teaspoon salt
1 loaf cubed Sourdough French Bread (see Index)

Pour wine into 1½-quart pan. Add garlic. Simmer uncovered 10 minutes. Discard garlic cloves. Combine cheese, flour, and pepper and stir into hot wine. Simmer mixture 10 minutes. Stir in kirsch, butter, and cream. Simmer for 15 more minutes. Season with salt. Serve immediately with cubed sourdough French Bread.

french bread fondue

ham snacks

An unusual snack to serve at your next cocktail party.

Yield: 10 snacks

**1 5½-ounce package
    buttermilk biscuit mix
⅓ cup sourdough starter
2 to 3 tablespoons water
½ cup margarine, melted
¼ teaspoon garlic powder
¼ cup sesame seeds
½ cup cheese spread
½ pound boiled ham, cut into
    thin strips**

Combine biscuit mix, sourdough starter, and water. Stir to blend.

Knead about 5 times on floured surface, with floured hands. Divide dough into 10 equal balls. Using floured hands, roll balls into oblong sticks.

Combine melted margarine and garlic powder. Roll sticks in garlic–margarine mixture, then in sesame seeds.

Place sticks on lightly greased baking sheet. Bake them 10 to 12 minutes in 450° F oven. Cool them. Coat sticks with cheese spread. Cover each cheese-coated stick with a ham slice.

salami tartare

A delicious snack for football-watching fans.

Yield: 4 open-faced sandwiches

**4 thick slices sourdough
    Caraway Rye Bread (see
    Index)
Butter
8 ounces party salami, sliced
    thin**

**1 green pepper, sliced into
    rings
4 raw egg yolks
Freshly ground pepper**

Toast the bread. Spread toast with butter. Distribute salami evenly among toast slices. Top salami with pepper rings and raw egg yolk. Garnish with freshly ground pepper.

sirloin puffs

Yield: 4 dozen

> 1 recipe sourdough Butterhorn
>   dough (see Index)
> 3 pounds sirloin steak, cooked
>   rare
> 2 cups asparagus spears,
>   cooked
> 2 teaspoons salt
> ½ teaspoon pepper
> ½ teaspoon garlic powder

sirloin puffs

Prepare sourdough Butterhorn dough. Let rise.

While bread is rising, cut steak and asparagus into small bite-size pieces.

Combine steak, asparagus, salt, pepper, and garlic powder. Toss to mix.

Punch down dough. Roll dough into ¼-inch-thick rectangle. Cut dough into 48 equal parts. Place about a tablespoon filling on each piece of dough. Fold dough over filling. Crimp edges. Place on greased cookie sheet. Let rise 30 minutes.

Bake puffs in preheated 375°F oven 15 minutes or until done. Serve them warm.

party dagwood

A hit at a teenage slumber party.

Yield: 12 servings

> 1 loaf Cuban Round (see
>   Index), cut in half
>   diagonally
> ½ cup mayonnaise
> 8 1-ounce slices American
>   Cheese
> 8 1-ounce slices boiled ham
> 8 1-ounce slices bologna

> 8 1-ounce slices roast beef
> 8 1-ounce slices corned beef
> 8 1-ounce slices Swiss cheese
> 1 cup shredded lettuce
> 1 tomato, sliced thin
> 1 Bermuda onion, sliced thin
> ½ cup dill-pickle slices

Spread bread with mayonnaise. Arrange remaining ingredients in layers on bottom half of bread. Top with remaining bread. Cut it into 12 wedges to serve.

132

whole-wheat rolled sandwiches

Yield: 24 party sandwiches

**12 thin slices sourdough
Honey Whole-Wheat
Bread (see Index)
13-ounce package cream
cheese
1 tablespoon milk**

Remove crust from thin bread slices.

Whip cream cheese and milk until light.

Spread bread slices with cream-cheese spread. Roll up each slice and fasten with a wooden toothpick. Wrap rolls in waxed paper and cover them with a damp towel. Chill them well.

Just before serving, remove toothpicks and cut sandwiches in halves. Arrange them on serving platter.

party stacks

Yield: 16 each

**8 slices sourdough Honey
Whole-Wheat Bread (see
Index)
½ cup butter, softened
4 lettuce leaves
½ cup mayonnaise
8 1-ounce slices cooked white
chicken meat
8 slices cooked bacon
8 tomato slices
16 olives**

Toast bread slices and spread them with butter. Cover 4 slices with chicken, spread them with mayonnaise, and top each with a lettuce leaf. Cover each with a slice of toast and spread with mayonnaise. Place bacon and tomato slices on top second slice of bread. Cover with remaining toast slices. Fasten securely with 4 wooden toothpicks. Cut sandwiches diagonally into 4 triangles. Arrange them upright on serving tray. Garnish with olives.

cornflake sticks

Yield: 16 each

2 cups all-purpose white flour
1 teaspoon baking soda
½ teaspoon salt
⅓ cup shortening
⅓ cup milk
½ cup sourdough starter
¼ cup milk
1 cup cornflakes, crushed
1 teaspoon salt
1½ teaspoons sesame seeds

Sift flour, baking soda, and salt together. With pastry blender cut in shortening until mixture resembles a coarse cornmeal. Add ⅓ cup milk and the sourdough starter all at once, stirring only enough to combine.

Turn out mixture onto lightly floured board and knead gently 5 or 6 times. Divide dough into 16 equal parts. Roll each part on the board with palms of your hands until it becomes a cylinder about 6 inches long. Brush them with milk.

Combine cereal, salt, and seeds. Roll each stick in mixture. Place on greased baking sheets and bake them in 450° F oven 15 minutes or until golden brown.

toast rounds

An inexpensive party cracker.

Yield: 5 dozen

1-dozen Sourdough Dinner
Rolls (see Index)
1 cup butter, melted

Slice dinner rolls crosswise into 5 equal parts. Place in single layers on cookie sheets. Brush them generously with melted butter. Bake them in preheated 275°F oven until golden brown. Turn bread and repeat process.

garlic toast

Delicious served with spaghetti and meatballs.

Yield: 1 dozen

**1 loaf Coffee-Can Cheese
    Bread (see Index)
½ cup butter, melted
2 teaspoons garlic powder
¼ cup sesame seeds**

Slice bread into 12 slices. Brush slices with melted butter. Sprinkle garlic powder and sesame seeds evenly over bread slices. Place slices under broiler to toast bread. Serve toast warm.

cheese crackers

Delicious with homemade soup.

Yield: 1 dozen

**1¾ cups self-rising flour
1 tablespoon granulated sugar
¼ cup shortening
½ cup sourdough starter
½ cup milk
1 cup grated cheddar cheese**

Blend flour and sugar. Cut in shortening until mixture resembles cornmeal. Add sourdough starter and enough milk to make a stiff dough.

Turn out dough onto floured surface. Knead in cheese. Knead 20 more minutes, then pound dough with your fists 5 more minutes. Pat dough to ½ inch thick. Cut it into rounds. Prick tops with a fork.

Bake rounds at 400°F for 20 minutes or until lightly brown. Serve crackers warm.

bread sticks

bread sticks

An inexpensive snack to serve on Dad's poker night.

Yield: 2 dozen

1 package active dry yeast
2 cups warm water
½ cup sourdough starter
2 cups unbleached white flour
2 tablespoons granulated sugar
1 cup butter, melted
2 teaspoons salt
3½ to 4 cups unbleached
white flour
¼ cup butter, melted
2 tablespoons caraway seeds
2 tablespoons poppy seeds
2 tablespoons coarse salt or sea
salt

Dissolve yeast in warm water. Stir in sourdough starter. Blend well. Add 2 cups flour; mix well. Let mixture rise overnight or about 12 hours.

Stir down sponge. Add sugar, ½ cup butter, and salt. Add about 3 cups flour to form a stiff dough.

Pour remaining flour onto kneading surface. Pour bread sponge on top of flour. Knead until all flour has been worked into dough. Continue kneading until dough is smooth and elastic.

Place dough in greased bowl, remembering to grease top. Cover dough. Let rise until doubled in bulk.

Punch down dough. Cover it with the bowl and let rest 10 minutes. Divide dough into 24 equal balls. Divide each ball into 2 equal parts; form each part into a thin stick about 6 to 8 inches long. Place sticks side by side and twist them. Repeat process with remaining dough balls. Place on ungreased cookie sheet. Brush them with remaining melted butter and top with one of the seeds or salt. Cover them. Let rise 30 minutes.

Place sticks in preheated 400°F oven in which a pan of hot water has been placed on the oven floor. Bake them 10 to 15 minutes or until golden brown. Cool them.

ham pizza

ham pizza

Yield: Two 16-inch pizzas

> 1 recipe Sourdough White
>   Bread (see Index)
> ½ cup olive oil
> 2 small cans tomato sauce
> ½ pound ham, slivered
> 1 teaspoon oregano
> ½ teaspoon garlic powder
> ½ pound mozzarella cheese,
>   shredded
> ⅔ cup Parmesan cheese

Prepare sourdough bread. Let rise.

Punch down dough. Knead about 2 minutes. Divide dough into 2 equal parts. Pat each dough piece into a 16-inch circle.

Place dough circles on greased cookie sheets and bake them in 450°F oven 12 minutes.

While dough is baking, combine olive oil and tomato sauce. Spread mixture evenly over the 2 crusts. Top tomato mixture with slivered ham.

Combine oregano and garlic powder. Sprinkle over slivered ham. Spread shredded cheese evenly over ham-and-spice layer. Top each pizza with ⅓ cup Parmesan cheese.

Return pizzas to oven. Continue to bake them until crust turns golden brown and cheese melts.

pizza deluxe

Yield: Two 12-inch pizzas

1 recipe sourdough Cuban
    Round dough (see Index)
½ cup olive oil
1 medium onion, chopped
½ pound fresh mushrooms,
    sliced
2 small cans tomato sauce
½ pound hamburger,
    browned

1 teaspoon oregano
½ teaspoon garlic powder
1 teaspoon salt
½ pound mozzarella cheese,
    shredded
½ cup Parmesan cheese,
    grated

Prepare sourdough Cuban Round dough. Let rise.

Punch down dough. Knead it 2 minutes. Divide dough into 2 equal parts. Make a Cuban Round out of 1 part. Divide remaining dough again into 2 equal balls. Pat each dough ball into a 12-inch circle.

Place circles on greased cookie sheet and bake them in 450°F oven 12 minutes.

Heat olive oil. Sauté onion and mushrooms until tender. Stir in tomato sauce. Spread tomato-sauce mixture over baked crusts.

Combine hamburger, oregano, garlic powder, and salt. Top tomato mixture with hamburger and spices. Spread shredded cheese evenly over hamburger mixture. Sprinkle with Parmesan cheese. Return pizzas to oven and bake them until crust turns golden brown and cheese melts.

pizza toast

Yield: 4 open-faced sandwiches

4 slices sourdough
    Whole-Wheat Molasses
    Bread (see Index)
4 hard-cooked eggs, chopped

6 ounces mozzarella cheese,
    shredded
2 tomatoes, chopped
Parsley, chopped

Toast the bread. Spread chopped eggs evenly over toasted bread. Sprinkle eggs with cheese.

Place toast under broiler until cheese melts. Top with chopped tomatoes and parsley. Serve pizza toast hot.

italian croutons

italian croutons

A pick-up for your dinner salad.

Yield: 1 quart

  **1 loaf cubed sourdough French
      Bread (see Index)**
  ½ cup butter, melted
  ½ cup grated Romano cheese
  2 tablespoons oregano
  2 tablespoons garlic powder
  1 tablespoon basil leaves
  1 teaspoon salt
  **1 teaspoon freshly ground
      pepper**

Toss bread cubes and butter, then toss them with cheeses and herbs until well-mixed.

Spread them on ungreased jelly-roll pan. Bake them at 250°F until crisp and golden brown. Stir every 15 minutes. Cool them. Store them in airtight container. They keep well for 1 month.

140

cheddar-cheese balls

Yield: 30 each

1 cup biscuit mix
½ cup grated sharp cheddar
 cheese
1 tablespoon mayonnaise

½ cup sourdough starter
 (approximately)
½ cup seasame seeds
1 tablespoon grated onion

Combine first 4 ingredients, adding only enough sourdough starter to moisten dough. Shape it into small balls.

Combine sesame seeds and grated onion and roll balls in this mixture. Place on greased cookie sheet and bake them in 450°F oven 8 to 10 minutes or until brown.

"devilicious" sourdough dunking bowl

Yield: 2½ cups mixture

1 package hot-roll mix
¼ cup warm water
1 egg, beaten
1 package sour-cream-sauce
 mix (1.25 ounces)

1 cup cottage cheese
1 cup sour cream
½ package French-onion-soup
 mix
1 can deviled ham (4½ ounces)

Dissolve yeast from hot-roll mix as directed on package in amount of water specified plus ¼ cup warm water. Add beaten egg. Blend well.

Combine sour-cream-sauce mix with the flour from hot-roll mix. Add flour mixture to yeast mixture; blend well. Cover mixture and let rise in warm place until doubled in bulk (about 45 minutes).

Punch down dough and shape it into a round loaf. Place in lightly greased 8-inch cake pan. Let rise again.

Bake loaf in moderate (375°F) oven 35 to 45 minutes. Remove it from pan and let cool on cake rack.

Blend cottage cheese and sour cream; add onion-soup mix and deviled ham. Mix well and chill.

When bread cools, cut an 8-pointed star, about 6 inches in diameter and 2½ inches deep, from center of round loaf. Cut center bread chunk into 24 to 30 cubes for dunking; toast them lightly. Just before serving time, place deviled-ham mixture in hollow center of bread. Serve with toasted bread cubes, or let guests cut "Dunking Bowl" in chunks to spread with mixture.

index